1 2008年，长城会七位创始会员合影。
   The seven founding members of GWC in 2008.

2 2010年，长城会早期会员合影。
   Early members of GWC in 2010.

1 2011年，GMIC北京闭门会议合影。
   A closed-door session during GMIC Beijing in 2011.

2 2012年，GMIC北京开幕式前合影。
   Before the opening ceremony of GMIC Beijing in 2012.

1　2012年，（小米总裁林斌抓拍）文厨和雷军摄于硅谷特斯拉工厂门前，等候马斯克会见。
Lei Jun and Wen Chu at the gate of the Tesla factory in Silicon Valley in 2012, waiting to meet with Elon Musk. Photo taken by Lin Bin, the President of Xiaomi.

2　2013年，文厨与李连杰、雷军、马化腾在GMIC北京合影。
Wen Chu with Jet Li, Lei Jun, and Pony Ma at GMIC Beijing in 2013.

1 2013年，到访的部分会员在长城会硅谷第一个办公室门前合影。
   Members in front of GWC's first office in Silicon Valley in 2013.

2 2013年，GMIC硅谷部分与会嘉宾合影。
   Speakers and notable guests at GMIC Silicon Valley in 2013.

3   2014年，GMIC北京闭门会议大合影。
    A closed-door session during GMIC Beijing in 2014.

1
2

1　2015年4月，GMIC北京会后所有工作人员合影。
　　Conference staff after GMIC Beijing in April of 2015.

2　2016年4月，GMIC北京会后所有工作人员合影。
　　Conference staff after GMIC Beijing in April of 2016.

1　　2015年文厨拜访诗人余光中，摄于诗人家中的厨房。诗人说，你叫文厨，我们就在厨房合影留念。
Wen Chu with the poet Yu Guangzhong in 2015. The poet said that since your name means "the kitchen of words", we should take the photo in my kitchen.

2　　2015年，文厨和滴滴出行创始人程维、猎豹移动CEO傅盛，在硅谷家中吃火锅，煮酒论英雄。
Wen Chu with the founder of Didi, Cheng Wei, the CEO of Cheetah Mobile, Fu Sheng, talking and having hot pot in Wen Chu's home in Silicon Valley in 2015.

1   2016年，文厨拜会TED创始人理查德·沃曼，摄于其家中书房。
Wen Chu visiting the founder of TED, Richard Wurman in 2016. Photo taken in Wurman's study.

2 2016年3月，文厨拜会以色列前总统、总理，诺贝尔和平奖得主西蒙·佩雷斯。
Wen Chu visiting Shimon Peres, the former President and Prime Minister of Israel and Nobel Peace Prize Laureate, in March of 2016.

3 2016年3月，文厨邀请王兴、何小鹏、刘成敏、张勇、郝义等进行为期七天考察以色列的活动。
Wen Chu, Wang Xing, He Xiaopeng, Liu Chengmin, Zhang Yong, Hao Yi E, and others on a 7-day business trip to Israel in March of 2016.

1
2

1 2017年4月，文厨前往英国剑桥大学拜访史蒂芬·霍金教授倡议科学复兴。
   Wen Chu visiting Prof. Stephen Hawking at Cambridge University, initiating the "New Scientific Renaissance" in April of 2017.

2 2017年1月，《文谈》第一次录制。（图中：俞敏洪、图右：原研哉）
   The first taping of "Wen Talk" with Japanese Designer Kenya Hara and Yu Minhong in January of 2017.

2017年2月17日—3月17日，文厨独自驾车从北京出发，纵横中原，途经17个城市，和大家"一起"开启中国的"科学复兴"之路！

From February 17th to March 17th, Wen Chu drove across seventeen cities setting out on a journey of New Scientific Renaissance in China.

1 2017年9月，GASA大学2017级学员硅谷合影。
The class of 2017 of GASA University Silicon Valley in September of 2017.

2 2016年9月，高山大学(GASA University)硅谷一期部分学员合影。
The first class of GASA University in Silicon Valley in September of 2016.

1 2015年，文厨拜访日本著名花道家假屋崎省吾。
Wen Chu visiting the famous Japanese flower arranging artist, Shogo Kariyazak, in 2015.

2 2016年7月，日本前首相鸠山由纪夫出席GMIC东京大会合影。
Yuko Hatoyama, the former Prime Minister of Japan, attending GMIC Tokyo in July of 2016.

不东

文厨 —— 著
宋小可 —— 译

中信出版集团·北京

图书在版编目(CIP)数据

不东 / 文厨著. — 北京:中信出版社,2018.4(2018.6重印)
ISBN 978-7-5086-8872-5

Ⅰ.①不⋯ Ⅱ.①文⋯ Ⅲ.①企业管理－通俗读物
Ⅳ.①F272-49

中国版本图书馆CIP数据核字(2018)第067206号

不东

著　者：文　厨
译　者：宋小可
出版发行：中信出版集团股份有限公司
　　　　（北京市朝阳区惠新东街甲4号富盛大厦2座　邮编　100029）
承 印 者：北京通州皇家印刷厂

开　　本：880mm×1230mm　1/32　印　张：9　字　数：150千字
版　　次：2018年4月第1版　　　　 印　次：2018年6月第4次印刷
书　　号：ISBN 978-7-5086-8872-5
定　　价：43.99元

版权所有·侵权必究
如有印刷、装订问题,本公司负责调换。
服务热线：400-600-8099
投稿邮箱：author@citicpub.com

不东就西，无问西东。
唐玄奘说，不取真经，不回东土大唐。

自　序

我曾偶遇芝加哥博物馆之梵高专展，惊讶于他的名画《向日葵》竟有多幅，原本以为世上只有那一朵著名的天价"向日葵"。不但如此，梵高几乎每年都给自己画一幅自画像。我端详他的一幅幅自画像，由衷为他点赞，其画技越来越高，用意用心，也越来越深远！

《不东》一书繁体中文版去年由诚邦出版集团在台湾地区首发，主要是由于忘年交诚邦何飞鹏社长的鼓励。他说你可以把自己过去的"千字文"（我戏称我的短文章为千字文，主要是因为水平有限，每篇在千字左右，想写万字文也写不出）整理出来70篇出版。一则过去十年，我周游列国，工作之余随手记录的点滴心得，就是移动互联网时代人和事的第一手资料；二则也可以作为我自己工作和生活的一份学习总结。

《不东》繁体中文版发行后，除了诚品书店，在其他书店是买不到的。我就自己送一些给朋友，居然很多朋友说还是蛮"将就"的，为什么不出简体中文版？有次我找到老朋友路金波，国内出版界的达人，他说可以出版，但最好是出中英文版，就有了大家今天看到的这本书。

至于为什么是中英文版，路金波没有告诉我具体原因，就如《不东》繁体中文版，何飞鹏直到今天也没告诉我为什么只选择70篇出版。

　　回到文章开头的话题，我想千字文一定会继续写，《不东》未来或许会有很多不同版本。就像梵高的《向日葵》和自画像一样，我会一直更新迭代，把整理出版《不东》看作鞭策自己学习进步的一个方法。

　　我没有深度，就努力拓展人生的广度，延展时间的长度。

　　最后感谢本书中出现的每个人，这是我们的故事！

　　是为序。

文　厨

2018年3月23日于耶路撒冷

目录

世界小邮差

我有一个梦想和女儿 003
不东 019
天下一家 029
千字文系列 041
想象力的故事 061
印度"网"事 067
硅谷"网"事 071
千字文迎郝义 077
心意、善意和天意 081
交流、交易和交心 089
地球上每个人来一次GMIC 099
日久之道 107
搭手 119
会神 123

"见"

"问"诗人余光中 129
"反省"李开复 137
写在"文心雕龙"开号 145
《世传》一：TED 创始人理查德·沃曼 149

不东 | UNIVERSAL POSTBOY

佩雷斯的世界和平　155

三"见"　165

三"诗"　169

卡尼奇达姆　175

天下无霾　185

寻梦环游记　191

化简为繁　195

鸟声、钟声和名声　203

世间再无霍金教授，时间永留简史传奇　207

GASA大学

GMIC重大发布：筹建民间NASA　213

GASA大学宣言　219

GASA大学颜色　225

GASA大学人物　229

GASA大学方针　237

GASA大学使命　245

GASA大学：人类的最高学府　249

致GASA大学2017级同学　253

再致GASA大学2017级同学　261

探索什么探索　271

目录

CONTENTS

UNIVERSAL POSTBOY

I Have a Dream, and a Newborn Daughter   004
BuDong   020
We Are the World   030
BuDong's Journeys   042
Story of Imagination   062
About Mobile Internet in India   068
About Mobile Internet in Silicon Valley   072
Welcome E   078
Faith, Kindness, and Providence   082
Communication, Transaction, and Connection   090
Everyone Comes to GMIC   100
The Long-Lasting Way   108

THOUGHTS AND REFLECTIONS

"Asking" The Poet Yu Guangzhong   130
"Reflecting" with Kai-fu Lee   138
Constructing a Dragon with Words   146
TED Founder Richard Wurman   150
Shimon Peres' World Peace   156
Three Things I have Seen   166
Three "Poems"   170
Kainchi Dham Ashram   176

不东 | UNIVERSAL POSTBOY

No Smog in the Air   186
Reversing Simplification   196
The Sounds of Birds, Bells and Fame   204

GASA UNIVERSITY

GMIC Major Announcement: Building a NASA for the Private Sector   214
GASA University Declaration   220
GASA University Colors   226
GASA University People   230
GASA University Guidelines   238
GASA University Mission   246
GASA University: Institution for the Highest Learning for Mankind   250
To the Class of 2017 of GASA University I   254
To the Class of 2017 of GASA University II   262
The Meaning of "Exploration"   272

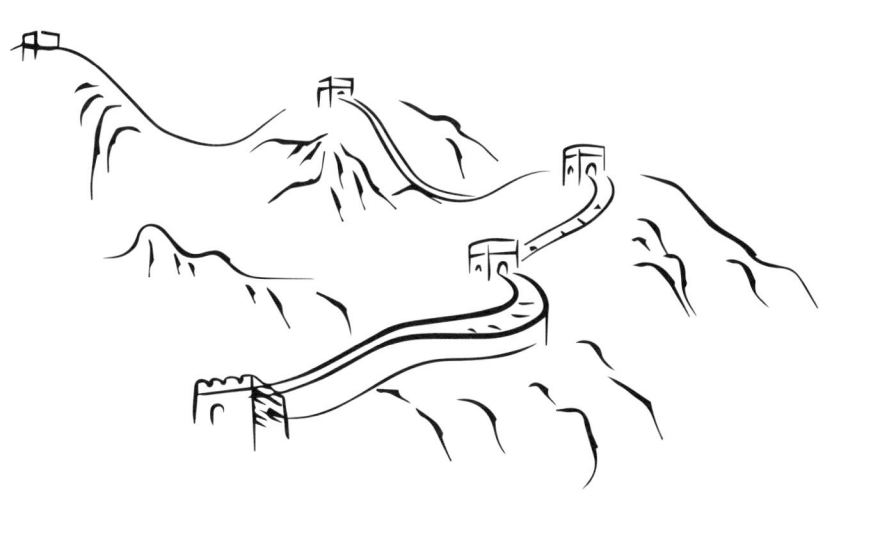

世界小邮差

我有一个梦想和女儿

长城会的同学们：

我来硅谷两个月了，一直想跟大家分享些什么，比如见闻、创新创意、碎片式的思考等。今晚终于有这个机会，来跟大家分享。

首先告诉大家一个喜讯，我很开心，今天我有了一个女儿！真的很美妙，我可以目不转睛地端详她一个小时。女儿再加上女儿的妈妈，现在我有一个更完整的"家"，这种家的感觉很幸福。

我们首先从"家"这个字分享吧。三年前，我创立了长城会。当时我倡导一个"小而美"的长城会，我们希望质胜于量，小就是美，而不是去一味地追求大而强。我也明确地告诉每一位被我"忽悠"进长城会的家族成员，我们很难"发大财"。长城会的故事很简单，我们去日本，希望帮助中日企业

I Have a Dream, and a Newborn Daughter

My GWC Family,

This is my second month in Silicon Valley. Since I arrived, I have been wanting to share with all of you my experiences here, innovative ideas I have come across, and new ways of thinking. Tonight, I am finally sitting down and doing just that.

First, I want to announce a piece of happy news: my daughter was born today! I am ecstatic. I can stare at her for hours without stirring. My family is complete now, with my wife and my newborn daughter. This is the most wonderful feeling on earth.

So, let us start our discussion tonight with this word, "family". I founded the GWC three years ago. At the time, I wanted a small but intimate club that valued quality over quantity, instead of one that pursued constant expansion. That was what I told each of the GWC members when I persuaded them to join our family as well: we were unlikely to become wealthy with the GWC.

多交流多合作，而且我们觉得应该更进一步，就提出了全球化。我们所做的工作都是些最基础的工作，办大会小会，组织各地考察，等等，这些事是发不了大财的。但是这三年我们大家一路走来，乐在其中。

这段时间，我在硅谷到处走走看看，本着多听、多学的态度去理解这个神奇的创新之谷。近来我问自己，为什么每个公司都要去做这个世界上最贵的"苹果"，而不愿意做个"橘子"，或者做那个"吃不到葡萄说葡萄酸"的葡萄呢？我们可以成为一个受人欢迎的"橘子"吗？让这个世界上喜欢吃橘子的人喜欢就好了。我们需要为此放弃些什么？我们如何与众不同？

我想跟大家分享我的第一个想法：建立一个"小而美的家"！今天有了更完整的"家"的我在想，我们长城会可以是一个家吗？一个公司对于人才的态度是优胜劣汰，那么长城会可以对所有成员都能永不放弃吗？对于一个家而言，家庭中的每个成员是无法优胜劣汰的。我的女儿之于我，无论她是聪明还是愚钝，我皆爱之。我的父母姐妹对于我，无论我是成功还是多舛，总是关心。我想挑战商业上的一些基本原则吗？是的，我想！我想换一种方式，但可以殊途同归。你可以对人才进行优胜劣汰，最终你获得优秀的人才体系。但我也认为长城会这个家可以自成体系，我们培养人，像对待家人一样培养成

不东 | UNIVERSAL POSTBOY

Our story was simple. It began with a trip to Japan, and a wish to promote communication and cooperation between Chinese and Japanese Mobile Internet industry. Subsequently, we decided to do more along this line, and to promote global communication and cooperation. Our work was simple too. We hosted conferences and led explorative trips around the world-again, not work that would make us rich. But in these three years, we have enjoyed our work together, which must mean that what we are doing has inherent meaning.

Since I landed in Silicon Valley, I have been avidly listening to and learning everything I could. I want to understand this magical land of innovation. I have also been asking myself, why is it that every company wants to become a huge and successful company, like Apple? Why are we not content to become something different instead, like an orange, or how about grapes? We could become something different, but still popular. So to that end, what do we need to give up? How will we differ from the Apples of the world?

Allow me to tell you what I believe in first and foremost: a small but intimate family. Today, when I finally have a complete family, I am thinking that the GWC is like a family as well. A company must do its best to find and employ the best talent, which is to say, only the fittest can survive. Along this line of thinking, would the GWC be able to keep all of its members forever, instead of keeping only the best? This is precisely why I believe we should consider the GWC a family instead of a company. We would never think of rejecting a family member who might not be up to our standard. I will always love my daughter, whether she is smart or not. My parents and my sisters will always care about me, whether I am successful or not. In this way, I must challenge this basic business rule of "survival of the fittest." I believe the GWC can operate on a different system. We should treat our members as family and nurture them as we would do to family members. We can start by choosing the best, but once someone is a member, we should never give up on them. Instead, we should invest our time

员，我们严格筛选人，从源头上做足功夫，只要选中就不要放弃，用时间、用家一样的亲情去培养他。我相信，最终我们一样能建立起优秀的人才体系，而且会是血浓于水的团队。我们为家做贡献，从没有主动要求家给以回报，长城会如果能做到这样，所得到的回报必定更加无法估量！

我们能为长城会这个家做些什么呢？南帝，你可以重新正式回归长城会吗？我想和你一起工作一段时间，让我们一起找到更好的工作方式，提升我们的工作技能。赵莎、瑞华，祝贺你们怀孕了！我很开心近来能听到这样幸福的消息。我们能为你们做些什么呢？可以为你们减轻一些工作负担吗？为什么你们怀孕休假工资要发月薪的一半呢？这正是你们更需要钱的时候啊！而且我们相信，你们选择在长城会孕育你们人生中最重要的家庭成员，你们将来一定会更爱长城会这个家，从长远来看，你们对长城会的爱只会更多！我们鼓励长城会的同学们都早点快乐地结婚，快乐地生儿育女。在这里我想告诉准备结婚的同学，我申请参加你们的喜宴，为此我可以从美国专程飞回去。事实证明，蒋丽娟的婚礼我见证过，现在她与我一起工作已十年；田丽的婚礼我也见证过，她是自长城会开创以来工作最久的同学之一。我觉得一个人愿意把一生中最美好的记忆与长城会分享，于我而言这是莫大的幸事！一直计划拥有一个孩子的同学们，赶快行动吧。有时候你想着应该准备得再充分些，但是世界上的事永远准备不完，就随遇而安吧。"老财迷"

and effort to help them. I believe in this way, we will end up with the best people anyway—we will have a team that is built like a family, because we gave without expecting anything in return. If the GWC can operate this way, what we gave, the efforts we put in, will be rewarded in spades.

So then, what can we do for our family? Nandi, would you come back to us? I want to work alongside you, and find a better way of operating with you, in order to upgrade our skillsets. Zhao Sha and Ruihua, congratulations on your pregnancy! I am so happy to hear good news like this. What can we do for you at this happy time? Can we take on some of your workload? Why would we pay only half of your monthly salary at a time when you need money? We believe, since you are choosing to have a child, one of the most joyous times of a person's life, while you are with the GWC, your whole family will love the GWC more in the future, more than ever before. We hope every member of the GWC will be happily married soon, and have children. I will happily fly back to China and attend your weddings. In fact, I attended the wedding of Jiang Lijuan, who has been working with me for the past ten years, as well as the wedding of Tian Li, who is one of the first colleagues of the GWC. How fortunate we are to be able to take part in the happiest time of someone's life! And those of you who have been planning to have children, hurry! I know you might think that you are not ready, that you should prepare better, but the truth is, you will never be ready, so just go for it. Even Warren Buffet said, the only investment that is guaranteed to be profitable is having children. And those of you who work overtime, if you believe that

巴菲特都说，这个世界上唯一不会损失的投资就是拥有自己的孩子！我也赞许在业余时间学习和提高自己的长城会同学们。如果你们认为加班时的工作内容并没有帮助你更好地学习和成长，那么就不要加班了，回去通过其他方式加强学习，谋求进步。记住，磨刀不误砍柴工。

从另一个角度看，我们其实是在用更长的时间跨度来看长城会的发展，不是一年365天，而是以一个家庭成员从出生后愿意为家庭所做的贡献来考量。所有按年计划的事业其实都很短暂！

我有一个小小的梦想，就是长城会像个家，可以很小，但一定有那么一点点美好的东西。我希望长城会在中国北京的那个家是一个有那么一点点理想主义、有那么一点点美好的地方！我们既然成不了那个最贵的"苹果"，那么为什么不试试做一个快乐的橘子呢？是的，我仿佛已经看到长城会在日本东京也有那么一点家的味道，一群日本人在夏野刚先生的感染下也能谈谈中日的恩怨情仇。今天，我在硅谷，我比以往更加坚信，"热眼向洋看世界，美中不足方才好"！

现在，我再给大家分享我的第二个想法，也可以说是我在硅谷学到的第二件事。我亲爱的同学们，我想大声告诉你们：我学会做饭了！真的很惭愧，三十多岁的人，居然一直不会做

working overtime has not helped you learn and grow, then don't work overtime anymore, but instead use that time to learn in other ways. It is always better to learn by doing instead of preparing.

In another way, if we can view the development of the GWC on a longer timeline, not in the space of a year, for example, but on the timeline of a family member's contribution after they joined us, then any yearly goals and plans would be very transient.

This is my "tiny" dream then, for the GWC to be a family, a small and intimate family. I want the GWC's China chapter, based in Beijing, to be a small family that is a bit idealistic, but also truly intimate. If we cannot become the most expensive "Apple" in the world, then let's try to become a happy orange. I can already foresee our GWC Japan chapter in Tokyo, and our discussion about the past resentments between China and Japan. And today, in Silicon Valley, I believe more firmly than ever that with a more globalized view, small imperfections are indeed, quite perfect.

Now let me tell you about my second idea in this area, or the second thing I learned in Silicon Valley. My dear friends, allow me to tell you proudly, that I have learned how to cook! I am a bit ashamed that I have lived for more than 30 years without learning how to cook. Now I know how to make rice and porridge, as well as many kinds of noodle dishes. When Lei Jun, the founder of Xiaomi, visited me in Silicon Valley, I took him to visit the office of the GWC

饭。我现在不但会煮米饭，还会煲粥，尤其是面食，我能做出若干品种，豆瓣葱油汤面、萝卜丝清汤面是我的拿手菜。这次雷军来硅谷，我单独带他来我们长城会硅谷的小家看看。进门后他说饿了，还没吃早饭呢。我说你想吃啥，我厨艺很棒给你做。他犹豫了半天。最后我给他煮了一份饺子，他的开心溢于言表。后来我们在海边谈起了生活的话题，谈了很多，都颇有点哲学的味道了。雷总说，怎么在这儿大家的脚步并不快，事也没少做，生活一样在进行，为什么我们一到北京就那么急呢？做饭其实是一种生活态度，生活很重要。我一路走来，发现自己其实忽略了太多生活的乐趣，比如尽量与家人一起吃饭，有时还要一起做饭吃，减少些无谓的应酬。曾国藩说"减少无谓应酬就是勤"，我想补充半句，减少无谓的应酬同时也是生活。顺便八卦一句，如果马云未来决定在美国待一年，可能有无数的理由，但其中有两条是陪陪老婆和送孩子去加州的某大学读书。长城会的同学，从某种意义上说这是另外一种建立和维护"家"的方式，有时候生活会给你更多源源不断的动力。我知道，生活过于安逸其事必不成，有曰："其为人也多暇日者，其出人不远矣。"我们的工作脚步真的太急太快了，我们可以慢些，因为可以走得久些，慢慢来，生活原来就是一剂良药。

第三个想法，开始读英文书。最近我买了我的第一本英文原版书《乔布斯传》（*Steve Jobs*），又是一件很惭愧的事，这

Silicon Valley chapter. When he arrived, he said that he was hungry, since he hadn't had breakfast. I said, why don't I cook something for you? In the end, I made some dumplings for him, and he was very happy. Afterward, we talked for a long time by the sea. Much of what we discussed took on a philosophical flavor. He said that even though the pace was slower here, everyone still managed to accomplish a lot while living life to the fullest. Why then are we always in a rush in Beijing? Indeed, cooking is more than just a chore. It is a way of life. I have been busy working, and ignored too much of the ordinary joys in life, like cooking and eating with my family, instead of always going out to dinner for networking's sake. The great Chinese statesman, Zeng Guofan, once said: "Diligence means networking less for networking's sake." I want to add to that, networking less for networking's sake means to truly live. If Jack Ma decides to spend a year in the U.S. in the future, he might have a million reasons, but one of them will definitely be to spend more time with his wife and his son, who is going to school in California. In some way, this means working to nurture a family, which will be your most constant motivator in the future. I know that if my life is too comfortable and easy, I will not accomplish much. As ancient Chinese wisdom says, "if one is idle all day long, then he must not be long for this world." I have reflected that some of what I've told you in the past might no longer be applicable. So really, we can afford to take things a bit slower, enjoy life, and learn the lessons life has to offer, so that we may be able to achieve more in the long run.

The third idea, let's begin to read in English. I purchased my first ever book in English recently, *Steve Jobs*. I am a little ashamed that this is the first English book I have read in English. I would be able to finish the Chinese translation

是我自己买的又真正读的第一本英文原版书。若说中文版，我想最多一周就可以读完了。现在一个多月了，英文版才刚起了个头。但是我想我会读完它，这对我来说更是一件挑战意志的事。我想起了若干年前，我练习高尔夫，别人一般三五个月就打得上手了，我却坚持了三年，天资真的有限，学什么都比别人慢几拍。为了长城会，也为了我自己，我决定练习英文，因为一个读四书五经，沉迷于诸子百家，酷爱中国历史的资质平平的中国人想去参与连接世界的一些工作。这其中有关意志，有关坚持，有关学习，更有关一个全新的视野！我跟马化腾、曹国伟和陈一舟等人都直接表明过自己的一个态度：雷军是我的"良师益友"！（我甚少把"老大"级的人物视为我自己的益友，有自我抬举之嫌。但是我发自内心地认为，雷总是我的良师，他也真的是一个热心真诚的益友！在我写这封信的时候，我收到一条他的短信，他恭贺我喜得千金！我都不知他是怎么知道的，可能是益群说的吧！）但是，我的后半句是"我爱我师，但我更爱真理"！这是亚里士多德对他的老师柏拉图说过的话。长城会的事业希望得到的不仅是雷军的支持，更需要大家的共同参与才更有意义！今天，这句话用在我学习英文的态度上是一样的，我爱我的祖国，我更爱真理，我愿意多一种视角、多一份胸怀去学习和了解美国，学习英文，运用英文与美国人民沟通和交流，这是一种基本的真诚！真正联结中美两国行业的源头就是这样一个基本的真理。我决心并准备带领长城会各位同学共同接受这个挑战！

of this book in less than a week, whereas it's taken me more than a month to read just the beginning of the English version. But I know that I will finish this book, precisely because it will be challenging. I remember that it took me three years to learn golf whereas most people need only a few months to learn, because I was not very naturally gifted with this sport. I learned rather slowly. Now, I am learning English for myself as well as for the GWC. I have always been an avid reader of Chinese classics and Chinese history, but now, I've set myself the goal of connecting the world. This is a goal that will test my determination, perseverance, ability to learn, and most importantly, my new, more globalized perspective. I have told Pony Ma, Cao Guowei, and Chen Yizhou, that Lei Jun will always be a great friend and a respected mentor of mine. (I rarely say that I am friends with such important people, for fear of coming off as bragging, but I truly believe that Lei Jun is not only my mentor, but also a friend who treats me with great sincerity. Just now, as I am writing this letter, I received a text from him congratulating me on the birth of my daughter. I don't even know how he found out!) But going along with that, I must say that even though I respect my mentor, I respect truth even more. This was what Aristotle said about his own mentor, Plato. I want the GWC to thrive, not only to garner Lei Jun's support, but also to give meaning to the work that all of us have done together. Today, I believe this applies to my learning English as well. I love my country, even though it might have been kept back by its traditional culture. But I love truth more, which means that I want to gain a fresh perspective by learning about and understanding the U.S., a country that deserves no less than my best effort. It is a basic form of respect to learn English and to use their mother tongue in communicating with the Americans. This respect will provide a great beginning to our work to deepen cooperation between China and the U.S. This is a challenge I am committed to accept, along with the members of the GWC.

My daughter is awake and crying now, so I will end this letter here. Even though I have not shared any amazing products or innovative ideas, or any meetings with

世界小邮差

伴随着孩子断断续续的吵闹声,这次给大家先分享这些。我没有与大家分享什么惊天动地的产品或点子,没有什么硅谷牛人观感,更没有所谓的美国"十里洋场"。我希望大家舒缓些、从容些审视我们自己,以及我们的长城会。希望大家看到的不是消极的态度、无聊的诉说,仅是我跟大家聊聊天。两个月了,也有点想大家了,想想12月要回去一趟,还有点激动。请大家相信我,我们发不了大财!既然这样,为什么我们不能选择让自己活得更开心些、更幸福些?我们不追求大而强,我们就要小而美,就要家,我们就把有限的资源(当然包括资金)放在我们小而美的家的建设上,我们稍稍有点不一样,如何?

自2011年大会以来,有些朋友给了我们长城会一些真心的称赞,同时我也能感受到我们一起奋斗的伙伴之间的一点点满足感!但是,近来我想得更多的是,我们长城会可以再多些"默默无闻"吗?最好从来没有媒体关注我们,从来没有被与我们所从事的事业不直接相关的人关注。我不是谦虚,每当我驾车在硅谷,我发现在北京我只有在天坛、地坛才能见到的巨木古树,这儿随处可见。大树见多了,就会觉得偶尔见到的几棵大树没那么重要。我深信,大器晚成!如果长城会是大器,她一定晚成!长城是由一块一块砖头垒起来的,几千年后的今天,每一块砖头就是一个风景,这就是大器!长城会就是要一个一个人、一个一个家地从移动互联网开始连接。我们不需要

不东 | UNIVERSAL POSTBOY

Silicon Valley giants with you, I do hope that this letter will inspire you to slow down, and take a gentler and more accepting view of yourself as well as our club. I hope that you don't consider this letter pessimistic, or boring. This is just some of my current thoughts, since I have missed everyone in the past two months. I am excited to go back to China in December. Please believe me, that even though we will not become wealthy through the GWC, we can make choices so that we become happier, more joyous in our pursuit of a small but intimate family. We can choose to invest our limited resources in building and nurturing our family. We might differ here.

Since the 2011 conference, many friends sincerely congratulated us on our work thus far, and we have felt some sense of accomplishment as well. But I have been thinking that it is perhaps best for us to work quietly for now. It would be best if we garner no media attention for now, and no one who is not working directly with us pays us any attention. I am not merely being modest. When I drive around in Silicon Valley, I have seen many ancient trees here that can only be found at historical sites in China. They are everywhere here, so they seem less precious. I believe that important things can only be achieved with time. If the GWC wants to be great, then it must take its time. We are connecting the world,

世界小邮差

人们关注文厨等创始人，我们甚至不需要人们关注长城会到底有什么意义。我们希望现在所做的，将来有人能受益。古代的帝王将相、芸芸众生所建的长城，是一个军事建筑，主要为了防御。今天的长城已超出防御的范畴，它是风景、是历史。今天我们大家建立长城会，在移动互联网，是为了连接。这是一个很单纯的信念，她的未来是什么？这有待世界来见证！

加州天空很爽朗，早晨的阳光很温暖，每当我沿着海岸边的碎石子路漫步时，阳光总是柔和地打在我脸上，我的心暖洋洋的；我又常会想起在斯德哥尔摩驶往赫尔辛基的游轮上，惊奇地仰望着那个我从未见过的世界上贼大贼圆的月亮；穿梭于日本的新干线和色彩斑斓的田野间，坐在松下幸之助的坟前仰望星空。我总是在问自己，我要什么？长城会要干什么？我可以让自己的心一直像这样活泼吗？各位长城会的同学你们想要什么？你们想象中的长城会是什么样呢？未来，我们长城会在阿富汗和利比亚的家该如何建立？

今天，我有了一个梦想和女儿，希望将来的某天，在地球上至少有100个国家和地区有长城会的家，虽小，但很美！

文　厨

2011年11月26日

one person and one family at a time. No one needs to pay attention to us, the founders and forebearers of the club, or to the meaning behind our club. All we want to accomplish is that in the future, our club will benefit many others, and become an integral part of their lives. Ancient Chinese emperors built the Great Wall for defensive purposes, but today, the Great Wall is more than that. It is a beautiful piece of our history and a cultural symbol. Today, we are building the GWC in the Mobile Internet space with a simple idea in mind: its future depends on all of us.

In California, the sky is clear, and the morning sunshine is full of warmth. Whenever I walk by the sea, and feel the sun's warmth on my face, I feel very warm inside as well. I also remember when on a cruise ship from Stockholm to Helsinki, I looked up at the biggest and roundest moon I had ever seen. And I remember too when in Japan, I sat by the mausoleum of the great Kōnosuke Matsushita and looked up at a starry sky. I am always asking myself, what do I want? What does the GWC want? Will I always be as vigorous as I am today? And, what do you all want, the members of the GWC? What do you want the GWC to become? One day, when we have expanded into countries like Afghanistan and Libya, what will our GWC family be like then?

Today, I have a dream, as well as a newborn daughter. I hope that in the future, we will establish the GWC family in at least 100 countries around the world, all adding up to our small and intimate family.

Wen Chu
November 26, 2011

不 东

亲爱的会员：

自7月11日首次全球移动互联网大会（GMIC）东京站后，一直有股暖暖的情绪在我心里流淌。今天，我决定写这封信给大家，或许这封信会是我这三十多年的人生中最重要的一篇习作。这封信酝酿于日本的古都奈良，我现在在硅谷动笔，我来自中国，原文是用我相较擅长的中文写就，或许英文版、日文版中的文字会因语言文化的缘故，被过滤掉一些信息和情感，但于我个人而言，这封信是用一份诚意和真心，向这个移动互联网世界尝试表达！

日本，古都奈良，紫罗花开。因筹办GMIC东京之故，我来日本，并顺道观光了奈良的千年唐招提寺，那儿有两座特别的唐代建筑，唐玄奘和鉴真两位中国高僧的主殿，这样的唐式建筑在中国一样可见，并无特别之处。但是，在殿上正中的两个汉字瞬间打动了我：不东！我感觉似曾相识，却不明就理。

不东 | UNIVERSAL POSTBOY

BuDong

Dear GWC Member,

I have felt a great warmth inside since our first ever GMIC, which took place in Tokyo on July 11. So today, I have decided to reach out to all of you, with what is perhaps the most important letter I've ever written in my thirty plus years. The germination of this letter took place in Japan's ancient capital of Nara, and I am now writing it out in Silicon Valley. Since I am from China, I will write in my native language. It is possible that some of my sentiments will be lost in the English and Japanese translations, but nonetheless I will do my best to communicate with the world of Mobile Internet with my utmost sincerity.

When I visited Nara in order to make preparations for the conference, violets were in full bloom. I visited the renowned Toshodai Temple, which is more than a thousand years old. On the temple grounds, there are two buildings in the fashion of China's Tang Dynasty, which honor two celebrated Chinese monks, known as Xuanzang and Jianzhen. Buildings like these are quite prevalent in China, so I didn't think much of them at first. But then I was struck by the two Chinese characters displayed front and center on these buildings. They said: "BuDong", the Chinese characters for "not" and "east." The sentiment seemed familiar to me, yet still elusive. "BuDong", does it mean then west, or possibly south or north? I tried to understand. In the end, I asked my Japanese colleagues for their input, because I thought the concept could not be understood with a purely Chinese mentality. They told me that in Japanese vernacular, the characters

"不东",就是西,也可能是南或北?我试图理解。后来我向日本的同事求证,这两个字已经不能完全用中国文化来思考和解读。在日本的俚语里,"不东"就是指不取真经不回东土大唐之意。

6年前,日本,时尚之都东京,时值3月,樱花盛开!这是我首次出国到发达的资本主义国家,在此之前,我没有在国外工作或学习的经历,所以,东京的一切对我来说都非常新奇。但是,作为一个中国的年轻创业者,兴奋和新奇之后,我发现我此行主要目的一无进展。我和几位中国的创业者此次前往日本的目的,是向当时日本领先的移动互联网同行学习请教。当时DoCoMo(日本移动运营商)及其I-Mode(日本移动上网服务)等商业模式引领全球移动运营商的发展,DeNA(日本移动互联网公司)、Gree(日本社交网站)和Mixi(日本社交网站)等是全球领先的移动互联网公司。但是,我们甚至都没有安排上一个简短的会见,其中原因或许很多,后来经我多方了解,关键点在于:信任!大到国家和民族,小到公司和个人,即使是在今天,你只要打开中日两国报纸,就会知道这依然是个问题!

我决定尝试缓解这个问题,至少在移动互联网这个新兴的行业,长城会就此创立!后来,我几乎每个月都会前往日本,带上一位来自中国的行业代表,用最朴素的方式,在日本办晚

spoke to the deep conviction of the Chinese monks not to return east to China without accomplishing their mission of obtaining the true Buddhist scriptures.

Six years ago, I travelled to Tokyo in March, at the height of the cherry blossom season. This was my first trip abroad to a developed, capitalist country. I never studied or worked outside China prior to this, so everything in Tokyo was fascinating to me as an ambitious young Chinese entrepreneur. But after my initial excitement subsided, I realized that my mission for this trip was not moving forward at all. A few other entrepreneurs and myself went to Japan in order to learn from our counterparts in Japan's Mobile Internet industry, which was ahead of China's at the time. DoCoMo was leading the development of global mobile operators with its "I-Mode" business model, and companies like DeNA, Gree, and Mixi, were also at the vanguard of the Mobile Internet industry. Unfortunately, we failed to arrange even a single short meeting with executives at these companies. There were likely many reasons, but the most important of which, as I found out only later, was trust, or rather, the lack of trust. There were gaps as big as the differences between our two nations, and as small as differences between two companies and two employees. Even today, if you look through Chinese and Japanese newspapers, you would know that these gaps still exist.

I decided to try to bridge these gaps, at least in the emerging Mobile Internet industry, by founding the GWC. After my initial trip, I travelled to Japan nearly every month. I would bring other industry leaders from China with me, and host dinner parties in Japan. I sincerely wanted the two sides to

餐会，每次都首先由我和中国行业代表介绍中国移动互联网行业正在发生的市场变化，以及一些生意机会和行业发展的趋势。半年后，日本同行开始与我们互动，尝试合作。我至今仍能回忆起，在那个时期，I-Mode模式的发明人夏野刚先生（后来成了我们长城会日本的董事长），在一次东京的晚餐会上，动情地指着DeNA和Mixi的CEO（首席执行官）等十几位日本业界同行说："这个中国年轻人来找我，说要加强中日两国行业的合作，多些信任。移动互联网是我们的新机会，你们应该参与和促成这件事。他的诚意打动了我，我决定帮助他！"这句话也常让我觉得温暖，激励我在未来的日子里一路前行。这也是为什么六年后的今天，我决定在东京举办GMIC，就是基于这样的信任，还有这份情谊。我相信所有的商业都将在这个基础上开花结果。

三年前，硅谷的秋，红叶尽染，阳光灿烂！我第一次来到被称为这个世界上最强大国家的美国，来到被称为这个星球上最神奇创新中心的硅谷。但是这个第一次来之不易，我被美国大使馆拒签三次！今天让我找个理由说为何被拒，我想或许还是因为有点小小的不信任。我再次迎难而上，长城会美国在硅谷创立！这后来，历史似乎重演，创新如硅谷，信任似乎又成了问题。在一次次北京—硅谷—北京的跨太平洋飞行中，我无数次纠结。记得第一次GMIC硅谷举办，作为一个行业会议，我们几乎第一时间向包括谷歌（Google）、脸书（Facebook） get to know one another. At each dinner, we would start by introducing the transformations that were taking place in China's Mobile Internet market, as well as business opportunities and development trends. After six months our Japanese counterparts began to return this courtesy, and wanted to find ways to work together. One of my most cherished memories took place during that early stage of the GWC. Mr. Takeshi Natsuno, the renowned creator of "I-Mode" and later the chairman of GWC Japan, pointed at me and told a dozen Japanese colleagues, including the CEOs of DeNA and Mixi: "This young Chinese entrepreneur told me that he wanted to strengthen the cooperation between the Mobile Internet industries in China and Japan, and to build trust between us. He said that Mobile Internet is a new opportunity, and asked for our participation and help in this worthy cause. His sincerity touched me, so I have decided to help him, even though deep down," His words of encouragement touched me as well, and I have thought about them often as I continued to work on these goals. This was also why that six years after that day, I decided to host GMIC in Tokyo. I wanted to build on this trust and mutual affection, and I believe everything we do will flourish on the basis of this trust and mutual affection.

Three years ago, I travelled to Silicon Valley in the fall, when red maple leaves were bathed in the warm Californian sun. This was my first visit to the U.S., the most powerful nation in the world, and the nearly magical center of innovation, Silicon Valley. The trip had been difficult to facilitate, however, because the American embassy rejected my visa application three times. If I were to guess at the reasons for this, I would have to say again that it was the lack of trust: the embassy officer mistook my enthusiasm for the trip as intention to emigrate. True to character, I refused to be deterred by this, and went on to found GWC America in Silicon Valley. But even then, even in a nation as powerful as the U.S., in a place as innovative as Silicon Valley, it seemed that history was replaying itself. Trust became a problem once again. I felt very conflicted each time I flew across the Pacific Ocean, from Beijing to Silicon Valley, and then back to Beijing

等全球行业引领者发出邀请，即使我心目中全球最具开放精神的谷歌和脸书，到我们大会临近举办的最后一周才确认安排一位重量级代表来参加。去年GMIC硅谷的闭门会议，我们在老朋友尤里·米尔纳（Yuri Milner）的家中举办，经由尤里的共同邀请，我们富有魅力而热情的脸书的马克·扎克伯格（Mark Zuekerberg）也是在会议临近召开前的几个小时，通知我们他将来参加大会的闭门会议。

即使今天，还是有人质疑长城会是否会成功，是否还会在硅谷办下去。从第一天开始，我就听闻"中国人来搞资源，搞得差不多就走了"。我很不服气，决定亲自来硅谷干三年。我们不但要把GMIC办下去，还要建成硅谷有史以来最成功的会员网络。我觉得硅谷现在还很不够全球化，更多中国人、日本人、印度人、以色列人及整个亚洲这个全球最大最具活力的移动互联网市场创新者应参与进来，还不能忘记非洲兄弟们，这才是真正意义上的全球化平台！

我较这个劲，就是想证明成功有多重要吗？而且就通过办个会？这对我来说，还算重要。但我认为，建立信任比成功更重要！一个基于信任的移动互联网的世界更重要！我梦想有一天，全球的移动互联网创新者能够基于信任，联结起来，团结起来，让移动互联网这一有史以来最伟大的创新力量改变这个世界，让世界更美好！这可以视为我对于挂在长城会各地办公

again. For example, we extended invitations to many global industry leaders to our GMIC in Silicon Valley, including Google and Facebook. But these companies, which I believed were the most open and globalized companies in the world, waited until the last week leading up to the conference to confirm their attendance. Last year, we held GMIC a closed-door meeting at the home of my long-time friend Yuri Milner. Yuri and I invited Mark Zuckerberg, but he too RSVP'd only hours before the meeting.

Even today, some would question whether GWC has indeed been a success. They would ask whether there will be more GMIC in Silicon Valley. From day one, I was told that Chinese entrepreneurs came to Silicon Valley only to get ahold of resources, and leave as soon as they had garnered enough. I decided to prove myself the exception, and settled down to work in Silicon Valley for three years. I not only want to host more GMIC, but I also want GWC to be the most successful industry network in Silicon Valley history. In addition, I believe Silicon Valley is nowhere near as globalized as it should be. There should be more Chinese, Japanese, Indian, Israeli and other innovators from Asia, which has the biggest and most vibrant Mobile Internet market in the world, as well as entrepreneurs from Africa and the rest of the world, taking part in GWC. Then and only then, would GWC become a truly globalized platform.

I do not work this hard just to prove myself successful, or even just to host GMIC, even though they are important to me. I believe building trust is much more important than success. A world of Mobile Internet built on trust is more important. My dream is that one day, Mobile Internet innovators around the world can connect and cooperate based on mutual trust, and enable Mobile Internet, which is the most powerful creative force in human history, to change this world and make it a more beautiful place. This is the story behind the GWC mission statement, which is displayed at our offices around the world.

室墙上的口号式使命的故事性叙述。

在奈良的唐招提寺,面对"不东",看着唐玄奘,我心里就想:你是唐僧,我是文厨!我应该干得更好,因我生逢移动互联网的伟大新时代!你的脚迈过小小的海峡已如此之难,我却可飞越太平洋!

这封信若就此结尾,我还是看到了一个极力想展示的"小我"。不求是中国的大水鱼,但愿做世界的小邮差。当我这样表达时,我看到有些同事在偷着笑,我知道他们在想,未来有一天,如果你真成了世界的小邮差,不就是大水鱼嘛。但如果是这样,这会是我人生奋斗路径上的另一种失败!人之常情,不喜仰望,居高而临下。但一颗小小的水滴,若能努力纯净,亦能折射太阳的光辉。我们中的"我",长城会今天这365位全球移动互联网里特立独行、卓越不凡的每一位会员,每一个"我",方能汇集成太阳的光辉!加州热烈的阳光狠狠地打在我的脸上,我不敢也不愿让心里的阴影停留太久。

我们可以吗?

文 厨

2014年8月22日于硅谷

不东 | UNIVERSAL POSTBOY

When I stood in Toshodai Temple, in front of "BuDong" and the statues of the monks, I greeted them silently in my heart: Xuanzang, I am Wen Chu. It was as if we were communing across the ages with our similar missions. But I also thought that I can do better, because I live in this most exciting era of Mobile Internet. It was difficult for them to cross the strait, whereas I can fly across the Pacific with ease.

If I end this letter here, it would be only a display of my own thoughts. It is not my ambition to become a major player in China. I would rather become a "Universal Postboy" who facilitates global exchanges. When I expressed this, some of my colleagues laughed. I knew what they were thinking: if I can indeed become such a "Universal Postboy", I would be quite an important figure. That would be a failure on my part. Perhaps it is only human to want to become personally accomplished, and to be able to look down on others. But I would rather believe that even a single drop of water can become as pure as possible, in order to best reflect the radiance of the sun. Today, I am but one of 365 accomplished members of the GWC, every one of whom is an extraordinary pioneer of the industry. All of us together, we can change the world. I am writing to you under the fiery Californian sun. As such, I am not willing to allow even a shadow of a doubt to linger too long on my mind.

Let me ask you: Would we do this?

Wen Chu, Silicon Valley
August 22, 2014

世界小邮差

天下一家

亲爱的会员：

　　游轮航行在加勒比海上，满天星辰。一首迈克尔·杰克逊的《天下一家》（*We are the world*），从Mini Jawbone（蓝牙音箱）中舒缓低沉地流溢出来。我决定就用这首歌名作为2015年最后一封信的标题，聊聊我们长城会小马奔腾过的那些日子，以及将要到来的喜气洋洋的美好时光！

　　这封信就像中学生作文，我愿此文终能"传世"！作文还是不作文，算是个问题；一个人作，还是一群人作，这才是真正的问题。我喜欢读任正非的文章，我发现随着他年岁渐长，他的文章越显深刻而严谨，但是我更喜欢他早期的《华为的冬天》《我的母亲》等文章，情真意切，激情澎湃。

　　我想表达什么呢？就从我们刚刚结束的GMIC硅谷开始说起。坦率地讲，GMIC硅谷已办了三年，不如意处依然不少，

不东 | UNIVERSAL POSTBOY

We Are the World

Dear Members,

I am sailing under a starry sky on a cruise ship on the Caribbean Sea. Michael Jackson's "We Are the World" is playing on my Jawbone portable speakers, so I have decided to use the title of this song as the title of my last letter to you this year, and talk about the GWC's rapidly expansive past, as well as our development in the future.

Even though this letter is written like a school composition, I hope its sentiments will last for a long time. The question is not whether I should compose this letter, but whether I will compose by myself, or with all of you. I like reading articles written by Ren Zhengfei, the founder of Huawei, and I think that as he aged, his writing has become more profound. However, I still prefer his earlier writing, such as The Winter of Huawei, and My Mother, because they were very heartfelt and full of authentic feelings.

What do I want to convey? Let's start with GMIC Silicon Valley, which had just come to a close. To be honest, after hosting conferences over the past three years, we are still far from perfect. Even so, I have decided to plan for the next

但是我还是决定规划出新三年计划，并且一分为二，2016年不但在硅谷办，还要办到纽约去。这是顺势而为，还是逆流而上？让我们从整体来看看。2015年的GMIC全球四站，9月的GMIC班加罗尔，首战告捷，超出预期。印度的行业领袖及其创新者，他们提出共建这个会议平台，首先因为他们国内自身行业发展，需要有这样一个国际视野的会议，同时这个会议也是他们打开全球合作的通道。7月的GMIC东京，磕磕碰碰，却被日本各大主流媒体拔高为中日两国民间行业交流合作的渠道，有益于中日两国友好，且被视为回馈的情意！因长城会七年前起步于中日的行业交流。5月的GMIC北京，机器人的讨论莫名其妙地被广泛关注，我们这个国家对这个世界充满好奇心。再回到GMIC硅谷，G-Trip（全球商务考察）从国内浩浩荡荡地来了一百多名会员，大家热情高涨，看到谷歌、领英、优步等观光团式的走访说蛮好，看到Coursera（在线教育平台）、Udemy（在线教育平台）等新型教育形态说蛮好，看到伯克利大学机器人实验室、3D Robotics（美国无人机厂商）也说蛮好。过去几个月，受GMIC北京机器人话题的热度影响，我走访了非军用领域的十几位世界级的科学家和教授。有几位会员说，GMIC硅谷此行，听吴恩达、克里斯·安德生（Chris Anderson，《长尾理论》《免费》《创客》三本书的作者，3D Robotics创始人）一席话，胜读一年书！

这是怎么了？我们团队尝试从三个层面来思考长城会的

three years in two parts. In 2016, I have decided not to only host a conference in Silicon Valley, but in New York as well. Is this going along with the current of our development, or against? Let's look at the situation as a whole. In 2015, we hosted GMIC in four cities around the world. The first was GMIC Bangalore in September, which went very well, better even than we had expected. Many Indian tech industry leaders and innovators suggested building this conference platform together, because in the first place, their domestic tech development needs a conference with a globalized view, like GMIC, which can open channels for global cooperation. GMIC Tokyo in July, even with its setbacks, was considered by mainstream Japanese media as a channel for cooperation and communication between the Chinese and Japanese tech sectors, as well as beneficial for the bilateral relationship between the two countries, because the GWC started seven years ago as a result of exchanges between the two sectors. In GMIC Beijing, hosted in May, our discussions about Artificial Intelligence became widely covered by the media and the general public, which also suggested that China, as a country, is full of curiosity for the world. At last, returning to GMIC Silicon Valley, our "G-Trip" brought over 100 enthusiastic members from China. They visited well-known tech companies like Google, LinkedIn, and Uber, companies pioneering new education platforms like Coursera and Udemy, as well as the UC Berkeley Robot Lab and 3D Robotics. They were impressed with all of them. In the past few months, influenced by the avid discussions on robotics at GMIC Beijing, I visited more than ten world-class scientists and professors in the non-military AI sector. These two robotics companies are but a small part of that industry. So really, our members are easily satisfied. Some members even said it was worth taking this trip just to listen to Andrew Ng and Chris Anderson (Founder of 3D Robotics and best-selling author of The Long Tail, Makers, and Free) speak.

What caused this? Our team considers the work of the GWC from three aspects:

工作：

第一，交流产生想法。我们组织各种形式的活动，大到GMIC，小到晚餐会，不大不小的会员年会、沙龙、名企学习考察等。交流可以启发人的思维，产生新的想法，帮助工作和生活。

第二，交易产生价值。在各种形式的活动中，由于会员彼此之间的互动，或者因国别区域的差别，这时候自然会发生一些业务层面的合作需求、投资和收购等，交易就产生了，体现了商业的价值。

第三，交心产生思想。交流和交易的过程，人与人之间彼此熟识。这种熟识发生在会员之间，同时跨越国界，熟识会让人更愿意分享。这个世界最精彩之处，就是人人都是情感动物，具有情感基础的分享才会越来越接近于真正的分享！真正的分享浓烈之时，心与心会碰撞出思想的火花。

我喜欢交流，我也喜欢交易的乐趣，但思想的盛宴是我的最爱！现在我们回到GMIC全球四站，印度的行业需要国际视野以及全球合作的通道，日本的行业需要民间交流渠道，中国的行业需要对这个世界的好奇心和对硅谷创新的学习。其实在我看来，隐含其中的都是一个全球化思想！今天的移动互联网时代，注定也是一个全球化的时代，人与人之间从未如此便捷

First, Inspire Ideas. We organized many different activities, including large-scale ones like GMIC, small-scale ones like dinner parties, and everything in-between like annual member conferences, group discussions, and visits to well-known companies. Through these activities and exchanges, we hope to inspire our members to arrive at new ideas, which will help our work as well as our daily lives.

Second, Create Value. Our activities promote cooperation between our members. Or better put, the need for cooperation naturally arises since our members are from different countries, including the need for business development, investment, and mergers, which will then result in business deals, creating value for everyone involved.

Third, Promote Thinking. As we communicate and cooperate, we are becoming more familiar with each other. When this process takes place between our members across national borders, it contributes to a sharing of different ways of thinking. This is why the world is an interesting place. We, as human, are naturally emotional, so it is when we share with an emotional basis that we can achieve sharing in the real sense, and promote real thinking.

I like such connections, and enjoy value-creating transactions, but a feast full of thinking is my favorite. Let's get back to the four GMIC around the world. The tech industry in India is in need of a globalized view and channels for global cooperation. The industry in Japan needs a channel for exchanges, the one in China is full of curiosity for the world, and needs to learn from innovation in Silicon Valley. From my point of view, I believe all of these needs are based on globalized thinking. Our age of Mobile Internet is bound to be a globalized age as well. We have never been so intimately connected with one another, nor have we wanted to be connected as badly as we do now. We live in a world where everyone is connected, and everyone's success is determined collectively as well.

地联系在一起，人类又是如此地渴望融合在一起，我们面对的是一个共生共荣又休戚相关的世界！

我上月去西班牙，顺道看了看哥伦布博物馆。我想，发现新大陆实质是地理上东西方真正开始连接在一起，全球一体化。之后，随着航海、航天航空、铁路和公路等交通方式的发展，世界各地的文明开始交融，互相影响，互为彼此。移动互联网，有时候我想它也是一种新式的"交通方式"，它以席卷一切的势能，改变我们的方方面面，全球化思想注定在今天移动互联网时代集其大成，修成正果！

2016年，我们长城会将顺全球化之势而为，由GMIC全球四站发展到全球十站。我们知道即使办个会，也会面临这样那样的困难，在欧美成熟市场里，办全球化会议有数十年甚至百年历史的比比皆是，短短几年的GMIC要向他们看齐，是何其难矣。当我讨论新年前往印尼、巴西、俄罗斯、南非、欧洲等国家和地区的计划时，还是听到像当初计划前往印度一样的提醒，有些地方比较乱，还有可能发生战争，还有可能对华人不友好，还有些所谓政治大环境变化问题，等等。我感慨，今天我还没有决定去朝鲜、阿富汗和索马里，而那些还算太平的国家和地区都不能去，全球化思想之光何日照耀这个星球？我不做，谁去做？今天不干，明天再干，明天是哪天？

不东 | UNIVERSAL POSTBOY

I went to Spain last month, and visited the Christopher Columbus Museum. I was thinking then that the discovery of the New World was the beginning of connecting the East and the West, the beginning of globalization. After that, the world began to connect through maritime and space explorations, and new modes of transportation like railway and automobiles, and different countries began to communicate and influence one another. I believe Mobile Internet is another new mode of "transportation." Its influence has changed every aspect of our lives, so globalized thinking will most certainly reach its height in our age of Mobile Internet.

In 2016, the GWC will go along with this trend of globalization, and expand GMIC network into ten chapters from the current four. We know that we will face many difficulties. For example, there are many globalized conference organizers in the developed markets that have operated for decades, even for the last century. It would be difficult for us to catch up with them in the shortterm. When I was planning my trips to Indonesia, Brazil, Russia, South Africa, parts of Europe, and Taiwan, I received the same reminder I did before I went to India: these places might be turbulent, war might break out, some might not welcome Chinese visitors, whereas others might be experiencing political changes. I received such reminders just by visiting what I considered to be relatively peaceful nations. What would happen if I decide to go to North Korea, Afghanistan, or Somali? How could globalized thinking reach all corners of the world like this? If I do not work on this, who will? If we do not do something about this today, when would we?

世界小邮差

今天，移动互联网时代，全球化是中国千载难逢的机遇，拥抱这个世界，友好地真诚地用心地呵护这个世界，中国融合世界，世界融合中国！

1492年8月3日，哥伦布和87名船员，驾驶"圣玛丽亚号""平塔号""尼娜号"三艘帆船，一路向西，乘风破浪。

新年快乐！

文 厨
2015年1月15日

自驾美国一号公路（Tips: Loncly Planet）

想了想，还是决定把这个攻略写出来，虽然我觉得有些不务正业，哪怕把时间花在GMIC销售展位上，多卖出个十万元的小展位也好。但是，我真的想写。有时候我问自己，我为什么觉得这个世界如此美好，一部分原因就是一段段特别的旅行！自驾美国一号公路，高铁穿越北海道夜幕雪景，飞行在印度各大宗教圣地，漫步在欧洲小镇观赏千年的教堂，航行在波罗的海、加勒比海数星星看月亮，不一而足，这其中有这个世界传递给我们的启示。

不东 | UNIVERSAL POSTBOY

Today, in our age of Mobile Internet, it is useless to wonder if we are becoming more powerful again. Instead, we should embrace this opportunity of globalization, embrace this world, nurture this world as if it is our own. China is a part of this world, and this world includes China!

On August 3, 1492, Christopher Columbus set sail toward the west with a crew of 87, on three ships named the Santa Maria, the Pinta, and the Nina. It was a journey that changed the world.

Happy New Year!

Wen Chu
January 15, 2015

世界小邮差

我曾经是捧着《孤独星球》的穷游一族，细想各位会员应少走些弯路，我决定写出这第一篇《孤独星球》。每年，我们一定要至少有一次十天以上的旅行，带着老婆孩子或男女朋友，亦可独自一人上路。这一次，就介绍我的刚好十天的年终旅行。由迈阿密开始，游轮经加勒比海南线，途经古巴、牙买加和开曼。怀念哥伦布，他发现了这些大陆。开曼群岛，长城会总部注册地，相信大家知道也有很多公司注册在此地。自驾，驶于美国东部一号公路，从迈阿密至萨凡纳，离开一号公路一段时间从维洛海滩至可可海滩的A1A（美国佛罗里达州公路）海中海岸线，很美。尽头就是美国国家航空航天局（NASA）的肯尼迪航天中心，去巨幕影城看浩瀚的宇宙纪录片，从大处着眼！璀璨的星辰，海阔天空的人生。离开肯尼迪航天中心时，我想如果有一天长城会要建立一个旅行者太空中心，我建议把基地选在连接太平洋和大西洋的开曼群岛。

驾车途中，听迈克尔·杰克逊的音乐尤好，他的音乐仿佛是为这片风景、这块土地谱写。

文　厨
马年最后一天海上动笔，结稿于文坊

千字文系列

千字文之东京行

刚刚翻阅《哥伦布航海日志》,我感慨世上的事皆机缘使然,这本日志若论文学性,可忽略不计,今天航行了多少里格,明天的航向纬度,但它是传世的记录。我又想起司马迁的《史记》,以及他的"究天人之际,通古今之变",一个失意的史官,用笔书写了一个个鲜活跌宕的人物传记。这些人真正谱写了波澜壮阔的历史画卷。我一直认为文章是末技,今天我却决定拿起笔来,这或许是我的宿命吧。

这次我请Snapchat(照片分享应用)的CEO伊文来东京晚餐会,就是想请他来聊聊"建立一个再现现实人生的虚拟世界"。曾几何时,我们不自觉地开始希望记录下自己人生的每个瞬间,却忘记吃顿饭睡个觉看段景,你当时想分享就分享,为什么一定要保存这一切呢?过去的就让它过去,该消失的就让它消失,这样也挺好。一个年仅24岁的创业者就凭这样一个想法创造了传奇。还有一次,我跟他说,阿里巴巴前CEO卫哲

不东 | UNIVERSAL POSTBOY

BuDong's Journeys

BuDong's Journeys—Tokyo

I was just reading Christopher Columbus' sailing journals, and reflected that everything in the world is up to chance. These journals are not at all literary, but instead recorded mundane things like how far Columbus' fleet traveled on a given day, and the direction of sailing for the next day. Even so, it is a rare record. I am reminded of The Records of the Grand Historian, and the author's conviction to tell all changes that occurred in history. He was a historian out of favor with his emperor, and dedicated his life to writing about many historical characters who made up a vibrant record of history. I had always thought writing is something I am not good at, but nonetheless I have decided to take it up. This perhaps is my providence.

I invited Evan Spiegel, the CEO of Snapchat, to a dinner party in Tokyo, so that we could talk about making a virtual world that is just like the real world. We often feel the desire to record each moment in our lives, but often forget to eat, sleep, and look outside. If you want to share a moment, then share it, why must it be recorded? Let the past stay in the past, and let what is meant to disappear, disappear. A 24-year-old entrepreneur used this idea to create a miracle. Another

跟我分享，马云问佩吉（Larry Page）谁是谷歌对手，佩吉说是美国政府和NASA，NASA干的事我想干，但航天是管制行业不让我干，政府里有些人才我付再高薪水再多股票也吸引不来。同样的问题，苹果的库克（Tim Cork）说，他的对手永远是苹果的上一代产品，因为自乔布斯以来，每一代产品都很难超越。他们都没有提到另外一家大家认为看似是竞争对手的公司。我也说了我由此的发散思考，我一直以为长城会的对手是国内外的那些行业会议，那么可不可以是联合国和奥运会呢？GMIC可以向奥运会看齐吗？它可以不仅仅是一个行业会议，也可以像奥运会那样除了更快、更高、更强，还倡导世界和平、公平竞技的价值观吗？GMIC是移动互联网行业的风向标和万花筒，它可以传递我们的使命——连接、信任和创新，让这个世界更多地连接，彼此多些信任，让创新的精神和力量惠及每个国家和地区的移动互联网行业。按此推理，长城会就是一个以民间的移动互联网为载体的"联合国"！连接移动互联网的领导者和创新者，就是连接了一个个"国家"和"地区"！今天每一个移动互联网平台或公司，几百万、几千万、几个亿甚至十几亿用户，就是一个个虚拟的"国家"和"地区"，这一个个"国家"和"地区"正在改变这个现实世界，力量惊人！"联合国"日渐式微，基于民间智慧自由组合的虚拟机构或许正当其时。伊文说，很多人认为他的对手是脸书，而他认为当前最大的挑战是手机软件的生态系统，这一系统本身安全吗？它其实充满着不确定性。

time, I asked a question that Wei Zhe shared with me. The story goes, Jack Ma asked Larry Page who he considers Google's competitor to be. Page cited the U.S. government and NASA. He said he wanted to do what NASA was doing, but space travel was an industry controlled by the government, so that he could not. There were also talents in the U.S. government that he could not attract with money or Google stocks, because they believed in their country. When asked the same question, Apple's Tim Cook said that his biggest competitor was always Apple's last generation of products, because every generation was hard to surpass. Neither of them mentioned companies that everyone usually considered to be their competitors. I reflected that I used to think that the biggest competitors of the GWC were industry conference organizers in China and abroad. But perhaps our competitors are the U.N. and the Olympics. Could GMIC look to emulate the Olympics? GMIC could become more than an industry conference, but could also advocate for values like world peace and fair competition like the Olympics. GMIC is a signpost for the Mobile Internet industry, as well as an advocate for our values to connect, trust, and innovate--make this world more connected, build mutual trust, and promote the spirit of innovation in the Mobile Internet industry in every country. In this sense, the GWC is a United Nations-like organization superimposed on the platform of the Mobile Internet. The leaders and innovators that connect through Mobile Internet are connecting nations. Every platform or company has millions or billions of users, so they are like virtue nations. These nations are changing the real world. In today's world, the real U.N. is becoming less important, whereas these virtual "UN" networks are perhaps on the cusp of flourishing. Mr. Spiegel said that many people would say FaceBook is the biggest competitor of Snapchat, but he believed that Snapchat's biggest challenge was the App ecosystem. Is it a safe system? It faces great uncertainties in the future.

世界小邮差

这次与日本业界的朋友聊天，普遍给我这样一种感觉，就是日本创新不力，人才往政府机关或大型传统机构去，图安逸安全，已经失去了"二战"后的危机感。我曾去过松下幸之助出生的那个偏僻的乡村——千叶和索尼盛田昭夫生长的那个没落的渔村，我相信当时那样的历史大背景是他们发愤图强的必然选择。

日本曾学习中国多年，今天保存了中国很多传统的东西，比如建筑、园艺、茶道、花艺和书法等。今年的GMIC北京和东京两站，我想把这些也挖掘挖掘，有些好东西我希望能找回来。日本有一个现象一直引发我的兴致，就是持久经营。一个小面馆、寿司店、糖果坊，都可以经营几十年、上百年，传承很久。有一家叫金刚组的家族企业，世代造房子、修造寺庙，已近千年，直追牛津和剑桥的建校时间，这种经营的韧劲和执着的信仰让人深思！

文 厨

2015年1月21日于东京

千字文之印度行

三个月前，我曾在印度工作加旅行27天，这次又专程来几天，未来几年我计划常来。我从三个层面理解印度。

不东 | UNIVERSAL POSTBOY

I spoke with some Japanese friends in the Mobile Internet industry. Many of them expressed the concern that Japan's innovation was not doing well. Many talented people have gone to work for the government or traditional corporations for stability, and have lost the sense of urgency that was prevalent after WWII. I visited the village where Kōnosuke Matsushita (founder of Panasonic) was born, and the fishing village where Akio Morita (co-founder of Sony) grew up. I believe their environment and time period made their hard work and subsequent success inevitable.

Japan had learned from China for many years, and still keeps many elements of traditional Chinese culture even today, including architecture, gardening, the arts of tea, flower arrangement, and calligraphy. I plan to look into these areas during GMIC Beijing and Tokyo this year, and bring back some of what we have lost. Japan's longstanding businesses have always interested me. A small noodle shop, candy store, or sushi restaurant, could operate for decades, even a century, and pass on its tradition. A family business called Kongo Gumi has been constructing houses and temples for close to a thousand years. Its history is as rich as Oxford and Cambridge Universities in the U.K. This spirit of perseverance is truly admirable.

Wen Chu
January 21, 2015

BuDong's Journeys—India

Three months ago, I travelled and worked in India for 27 days. I am returning for a few days this time, and plan to come to India often in the next few years. I see India from the following three perspectives:

世界小邮差

第一，国家。印度很快会成为世界第一人口大国，现正是百废待举、万象更新时，新一届的莫迪政府务实进取，致力发展经济与民生。从世界范围看，印美注定越走越近，地缘政治经济发展正当其时。中印关系也必须前行，真正的亚洲世纪需要中印这两个人口大国的作为。可以说，印度被中美共同需要，这样的局面印度可谓乐见其成。总体来说，美印合作会走在中印之前。英语在印度相当于国内的普通话，是通用语言，谷歌是印度首选的信息搜索平台，脸书和推特（Twitte）是主流社交网站。微软和谷歌等一批美国公司里，印度裔高管蔚然成风，号称占领硅谷。两国合作基础厚实，未来一二十年，印度将迎来美国战略层面给以支持的经济红利。我国包括海上丝绸之路、高铁计划等在内的国家战略需要印度，合作也要往深处做文章，这对印度而言也是更多利好。

第二，文化。印度和中国都是文明古国，历史悠久，文化博大精深。尤其难得的是宗教信仰在印度深入人心，百分之八十以上人信仰印度教，佛教也发源于此，人多有敬畏之心。反思国内今天的假货泛滥、生态环境堪忧等问题，就是因为有一部分人拜金至上，少了敬畏之心。这也是为什么我们现在要呼唤传统，反思一味追求GDP（国内生产总值）导致经济过载的问题。我们需要重塑文化，建立起经济发展后的真正的大国自信。甘地式人物的出现以及这个国家经营多年的民主政治，具有长治久安的发展预期。

First, Nation. India will soon become the nation with the biggest population in the world. This is a great time of transition. The new government is practical and actively making reforms, building more schools than temples, and working hard to develop its economy and improve the lives of its people. On a global scale, India and the U.S. will become closer geopolitically and economically. China and India will move forward in unison too. A real "Century of Asia" requires cooperation between China and India. In fact, both China and the U.S. need India, which is a situation India quite likes. In general, U.S.-India relation will precede China-India relation. English is spoken widely in India. Google is India's preferred search engine. FaceBook and Twitter are its mainstream social media websites. There are many Indian executives in American companies like Google and Microsoft. Some might say Indians have taken over Silicon Valley. These two countries have a solid foundation of cooperation, and India will see economic profits from strategic supports extended by the U.S. in the next few decades. China needs India to realize its "21st Century Maritime Silk Road" initiative and high-speed railway plans, so cooperation between these two countries must deepen, which will prove beneficial for India as well.

Second, Culture. Both China and India have long histories and two of the oldest and richest cultures in the world. India in particular, has kept its religious faith. More than 80% of Indians believe in the Hindu religion, and Buddhism originated from India, so most Indians have a deep respect for the divine. Unfortunately, in China, fake products are rampant, and the environment is getting worse. This is precisely because many Chinese lack a faith system and a respect for the divine, and are very materialistic. So we need to respect traditional culture, and reflect on our single-minded drive for GDP growth. We need to renew our traditional culture, and regain our confidence as a large country after we have succeeded in economic growth. India will profit in the long-term from great leaders like Mahatma Gandhi and its many years of democracy.

第三，移动互联网。具体到移动互联网的生意层面上，我感受到难得的好气象。印度移动互联网的这批创业者积极阳光，年轻有活力。目前印度最大的电商平台Flipkart创始人萨钦（Sachin Bansd），在自家的平房里从一本一本书卖起，勤劳朴实，积极进取，憨厚阳光。我与他仅相交几次，对其谦和坦诚深为敬服，我视其为长城会印度合作之首选人物。此外，像最大的移动广告平台InMobi、有印度支付宝之称的Paytm等公司的CEO视野开阔，激情四射，有全球思维；电商平台Snapdeal、有印度滴滴打车之称的Olacabs等在内的一批移动互联网企业创始人皆不到三十岁，年富力强，斗志昂扬。这俨然像我国互联网发展早期的那批人那样生机勃勃，他们会成为印度移动互联网未来的领袖和创新引领者，我们现在跟他们合作，就是跟印度这个国家的未来商业领袖合作，未来可期。或者投资他们，事实上孙正义、尤里·米尔纳和国内阿里巴巴已经重资下注。以上各位，2015年4月GMIC北京我已一一发出邀请，将会齐聚北京城。未来，回顾中印两国移动互联网行业合作的历史，这也是一次值得称道的历史小聚！

文　厨

2015年2月7日

不东 | UNIVERSAL POSTBOY

Third, Mobile Internet. I am optimistic for the Mobile Internet sector. India's Mobile Internet has seen the rise of a group of young and talented entrepreneurs. Flipkart's Sachin Bansal started by selling books from his house, and grew his business steadily and practically. I have only met him a few times, and was very impressed with his humility and honesty. He is my top pick for collaboration with the GWC in India. In addition, CEOs of InMobi, the biggest mobile advertisement platform, and Paytm, India's version of AliPay, are passionate entrepreneurs with a global mindset; Founders of E-Commerce platform Snapdeal, India's equivalent of Uber, and many others, are less than thirty-years-old. They are energetic leaders with great visions in mind. They reminded me of the earliest generation of Internet entrepreneurs in China, and will certainly become leaders in India's Mobile Internet space. In collaborating with them, we are collaborating with India's business leaders of the future. If we invest in their companies, we would be like Masayoshi Son, Yuri Milner and Alibaba who had the foresight to invest already. I have invited the above-mentioned innovators to GMIC Beijing in April. They will gather in Beijing, which should prove to be a historical gathering for the future collaborations of the Mobile Internet industries of India and China.

Wen Chu
February 7, 2015

千字文之迪拜行

迪拜本身是一个梦想实践的见证，一座沙漠中的城市，一个人的欲望的释放地。

迪拜七星级帆船酒店是建在海上永远的帆船，全球最大的音乐喷泉每晚奏响水的乐章，全球最大的购物中心撩起人的物质欲望。我在世界第一高楼哈利法塔仔细看了看它的建造历史，从第一天修造开始，"最高"就是她在这个世界的诉求，她的地基是一座藏于地下的摩天大楼，以超越上海金贸大厦、吉隆坡双子星座、台北101大楼为建造目标。据说在建造期间，迪拜听说有城市要以它的计划高度新建一座更高的大楼，他们就公开放狠话，"我们的大楼塔尖可以自动升降，无论你的大楼多高，我们塔尖将升得比你更高"，逼人作罢。这是人类比高的典范，它创造了人类建筑史上的奇迹，这么一个浩大工程凝聚了一个全球庞大团队的集体智慧的结晶。这一人类朴素之"最"的想法，也在情理之中，放眼我们这个世界，最高、最大、最快、最远、最强等，处处可见，多受尊重。

拿我来说，我私下对人讲，我想把长城会做成最久的组织。有人说不在乎天长地久，只在乎曾经拥有。我总觉得还是天长地久踏实。我思考最多的就是长城会的久，怎么久久地活着。长城会的使命是连接全球移动互联网的创新者，彼此信

不东 | UNIVERSAL POSTBOY

BuDong's Journeys—Dubai

Dubai itself is the realization of a dream. It is a city in the desert, the fulfilment of one person's desire.

The Burj Al Arab is a sail that is always taut on the sea. The biggest musical fountain in the world plays every night. The biggest shopping center in the world makes everyone want to shop. I stood on the tallest manmade building in the world, the Burj Khalifa, and read over its history. From the first day, the Burj Khalifa wanted to be the tallest in the world. Its foundation is a skyscraper below ground, taller than Jin Mao Tower in Shanghai, Petronas Tower in Kuala Lumpur, and Taipei 101. During its construction, another city said it would build a tower taller than the planned height of the Burj Khalifa. The builders of the Burj Khalifa responded that it would have a retractable tip, so that it would always be taller. It is a prime example of the competitiveness of mankind, and a miracle in our history of construction. It is also the fruit of the collective wisdom of a global team. This desire to be the tallest is understandable. The tallest, biggest, fastest, strongest and furthest feats are found everywhere, and are usually very respected.

I personally want to make the GWC the longest running organization. Some might say that as long as something existed once, it does not matter whether it lasts forever. But I would rather the GWC lasts forever. This is something I think about a lot--how can I ensure the GWC's long flourishing. Our mission is to connect Mobile Internet innovators around the world, build their mutual trust,

任,让创新惠及全球。连接这一使命,我想也就几十年,随着移动互联网的加速发展,创新者连接就越来越容易。我们在印度办GMIC,几位印度业界大佬鼎力相助,说我们要很快把GMIC班加罗尔办得比已是几万人的GMIC北京更大更成功。印度市场够大,未来可能比肩中国,几位大佬在印度市场上一言九鼎,比当初我们在北京起步时大背景大环境要好。但后来我在印度工作生活了27天后,发现印度这个国家当前最大的问题可能是贫穷,多带些创新的思想、产品、技术等去印度,多宣传创新公司和创新教育平台等更有益于推动解决这个国家的贫穷问题。其实质是长城会在印度的长久之道,有时候事情没有错,次序错了,结果迥异。

我认为创新在较长的时间内是一直被需要的,一百年?我还是不踏实。我就继续去琢磨那些活得久的组织,比如达沃斯和奥运会,我发现它们的全球顾问委员会是个汇集众智的好办法,它们能活得久需要众人智慧。我琢磨近千年的家族企业——日本的金刚组和牛津大学,金刚组家族一代传一代,是为寺庙修造房子,是佛教的因,佛教一直兴盛才一直有房子修造。而牛津大学有基督教的果。我又琢磨基督教和佛教,发现这两个宗教好像是目前全球化做得最好的组织。这个发散有点长,可见最久之心有多强烈。

回到我在哈里法塔上的那个最高发"问",最高、最大、

and allow innovation to benefit the whole planet. This mission will take a few decades, and with the advent of Mobile Internet, will become easier. When we hosted a conference in India, we were fortunate to have help from a few Indian tech giants. They said that they wanted to make GMIC Bangalore bigger than GMIC Beijing, which has tens of thousands in attendance. I trusted that the Indian market is big enough to achieve this, and has a better entrepreneurial environment than Beijing when we first started. But after working in India for 27 days, I found that the biggest problem India is facing is poverty. It needs more innovative thoughts, products, and technology, as well as innovative companies and platforms to help solve its poverty problem. If we can accomplish this, then we can last for a long time in India. It is a simple question of priority.

I believe that innovation will be relevant for a long time. Maybe a hundred years? But I am still not assured, so I continued to study organizations that have flourished for a long time, like Davos and the Olympics. I found that their global committees are a good way to gather the wisdom of many, and their survival depended on this wisdom. I also studied the Japanese company, Kongo Gumi, and Oxford University. Kongo Gumi has repaired temple buildings for generations. Buddhism flourished, so that Kongo Gumi had plenty of work over the centuries. Oxford University flourished thanks to Christianity. I turned to Buddhism and Christianity then, and realized that they are the organizations that have globalized best in the world. This was a long thought process, a testament of my strong desire for the GWC's longevity.

Let's return to the Burj Khalifa and its desire to be the tallest. Being the tallest, biggest, fastest, strongest, and most long-lasting, these qualities are easily quantifiable and prompt competitiveness. But is that really a good thing? I

最快、最好、最强和最久,这些毕竟可量化,所以在俗世凡尘中,便于竞相追逐。但是,这个世界这样真的好吗?行文至此,我突然想起了一句大家耳熟能详的时髦话:"让世界更美好!"最美、最好、最美好,这个难以量化,但更美更好更美好是可以在比较中前进的。如果我们能"让世界更美好",每天更美好一点,每件事更美好一点,每个人更美好一点,就是一切之"最"也都有意义,这颗初心不忘,或许方得始终。

文 厨

2015年2月17日

千字文之巴西行

"纸上得来终觉浅,绝知此事要躬行。"第一次来南美,第一次来巴西。来之前,网上了解,听人介绍,对这里略知一二。但实地考察,见微知著,感受不同。

里约热内卢,海风和煦,人情闲暇;圣保罗闹市,晚上七点,人迹寥寥。就其行业而言,看似在转换爆发节点,其实还是在基础建设阶段。手机厂商、移动网络带宽服务商、运营商等可以有所作为,但内容服务、娱乐和移动商务等仍需时日。GMIC要来巴西,此情此景,颇让我一筹莫展。但新兴大国,

remember suddenly that sentence: "Make the world a better place." Better, best, these are qualities that are more difficult to quantify, but prompt us to move forward. If every day, we can make the world a better place. If with everything we do, we can make the world a better place. If all of us, can make the world a better place. Then what we do would be truly meaningful. If we do not forget this mission, then the GWC will indeed have a chance to be long-lasting.

Wen Chu
February 17, 2015

BuDong's Journeys—Brazil

A Chinese poem said, "Nothing can be learned truly unless you do it yourself." This is my first trip to South America, to Brazil. I have heard others talk about this country, and read about it online, but my first-hand impression of the country, once I have arrived, is very different.

Rio de Janeiro has a calm sea breeze. Its people are relaxed. At 7p.m. in Sao Paulo, the streets are sparsely populated. Its Mobile Internet industry may seem on the verge of exploding, but in reality the country is still building its infrastructure. There are opportunities for cell phone manufacturers, Mobile Internet and broadband service providers and operators, but content, entertainment, and mobile business industries still need more time to develop. This situation will make GMIC's work in Brazil a bit difficult, but nonetheless, Brazil is an emerging economy with a sizeable market. Its importance is not to be doubted.

市场大势,毋庸置疑。

长城会使命——连接创新,彼此信任,从何着手?无意间一则消息,启发了我的思考。2016年7月,里约奥运,却是机遇!我请同事朋友立即联络里约市政府,GMIC明年与里约奥运会合作,搭趟便车,从开幕式、关键场次比赛到闭幕式,我们组织大家来看赛事,包上几个小专场。同期,奥运会开幕前先召开GMIC,巴西行业不温,我们帮着升温;巴西市场不火,我们帮着点把火。

2014年,GMIC硅谷,国内浩浩荡荡来了100多位长城会会员,但硅谷是全球创新中心,这样的场景如何复制到全球?GMIC北京,我不担心,北京是全球移动互联网市场中心,多年积淀,大家乐意来。有时候我反倒担心,大家期待越来越高,过犹不及,盛名之下,其实难副。GMIC班加罗尔,是又一个潜在的印度市场中心,预期很吸引人。巴西这个奥运的点,或许盘活了局,如何打开未来长城会在巴西发展的面?念念不忘,必有回响。刚说GMIC的"对手"是奥运会,现在就从合作开始,今年练练兵,明年好好干,后年接过奥运大旗,慢慢学习它的世界和平公平竞技的伟大理想,践行长城会创新世界彼此信任的小小心愿。二三十年后,奥运再次回归巴西,GMIC提前从容让个道,道声欢迎老朋友!GMIC巴西三年战略,长城会巴西30年的种子。

不东 | UNIVERSAL POSTBOY

Since the GWC's mission is to connect innovators, where should we start in Brazil? A piece of news I heard inspired my thoughts. Brazil will host the Olympics next July, which will be an opportunity for us. I asked the team to contact the Rio government and proposed cooperation between the Olympics and GMIC next year. We will also organize team outings to the Olympics' opening and closing ceremonies, as well as important matches. GMIC will be hosted before the Olympics. We will help to garner interest in the Mobile Internet industry and fan the flame for its faster development.

More than 100 Chinese GWC members visited GMIC Silicon Valley in 2014. But Silicon Valley is known as the center of global innovation. How do we replicate this avid interest around the world? I am not worried about GMIC Beijing. Beijing is the center of the global Mobile Internet market. Everyone is interested in attending the Beijing conference. If anything, I worry that people's expectations would be too high, and it would be hard work to meet those expectations. GMIC Bangalore will be the center of attention for the Indian market, so its attendance is assured. Brazil's upcoming Olympics will help us and let GMIC build a solid start in the country, instead of competing with us. We will start with cooperation and work hard next year, and every year after. Instead of competing, we will take on the torch of the Olympics, learn from its ideal of peaceful and fair competition, and realize the GWC's mission of building mutual trust in the world of innovation. In a few decades, when the Olympics returns to Brazil, GMIC will be there to welcome an old friend. The strategic goal of GMIC over the next three years will be to sow the seed for the GWC for the next three decades.

世界小邮差

　　同一颗种子，不同的土壤，浇灌不一样的水和养分。想起GMIC班加罗尔，原本是一颗更大更成功的种子，但印度的贫穷现状警示我，若能基于这一点播种，就不是三五年，而是三五十年！更大更成功三五年就够了，例如因行业过火急速生长的GMIC北京就好似越来越大，越来越成功。但印度想摆脱贫穷，没有三十年的改革开放，不可能解决曾经的贫穷问题。

　　长城会就按这样的心播种，就循这样的情融入每一片土地，放下速成，回归寻常。三十年巴西长城会，三十年印度长城会，我不知道硅谷创新之火能燃烧多久，但我确信，长城会起始的本心，中日两个行业因连接需要而渴望建立的信任，或许是百年的种子。我不知道这是长城会的幸运还是这个世界的不幸。让这个世界建立彼此信任，可能比消灭贫穷还难！待续。

文　厨
2015年3月16日

不东 | UNIVERSAL POSTBOY

The same seed, sown into different lands, will yield something different. GMIC Bangalore started bigger and better, but India's poverty problem made me realize that we needed to think of our work on a timeline of decades instead of years. To be successful requires a shorter timeline—GMIC Beijing has become bigger and better already over the last few years. But it will take decades for India to be lifted out of poverty, just like China experienced 30 years of reform before it was out of poverty.

The GWC will be patient with its seeds in every land. We will plan for three decades in Brazil and India. How long will the enthusiasm for innovation in Silicon Valley last? I believe, as long as the GWC does not lose track of its original mission to build mutual trust, it will enjoy a long time of flourishing. That would be lucky for us indeed. Perhaps building mutual trust will be even more difficult than eradicating poverty. Onward.

Wen Chu
March 16, 2015

世界小邮差

想象力的故事[①]

2015年初,我去台湾地区拜访了当时年届88岁的著名诗人余光中。我问诗人,什么是他认为人生中最为重要的。他用"想象力、想象力、想象力"重复三次向我进行了强调。

我想起长城会创立的早期,我在新浪微博上公开写出这些名字:乔布斯,施密特(Eric Schmidt),马云,马化腾,雷军,孙正义,夏野刚,蔡明介。我认为他们是引领全球移动互联网发展的领导者。我希望能邀请他们到GMIC,今天他们中有一半来过GMIC。腾讯创始人马化腾是我们长城会投资人,小米创始人雷军和I-Mode发明人夏野刚两位先生还是我心目中的创业老师,前者是我的第一个天使投资人并出任过三年长城会董事长,后者如今是我们长城会日本董事长。

我看,这可能算是第一个有关"想象力"的长城会故事。

---

① 本文是GMIC2015班加罗尔站的演讲稿。

不东 | UNIVERSAL POSTBOY

Story of Imagination[1]

At the beginning of this year, I visited the 88-year-old poet, Yu Guangzhong. I asked him, what he valued most in life. He said, "Imagination, Imagination, Imagination", repeating three times to emphasize his point.

In the early days of the GWC, I wrote a list of names on Weibo: Steve Jobs, Eric Schmidt, Jack Ma, Pony Ma, Lei Jun, Masayoshi Son, Takeshi Natsuno, and Tsai Ming-kai, because I believed they were the leaders of the Mobile Internet industry. I wanted to invite them to GMIC. Today, over half of them have already participated in GMIC. In addition, Pony Ma is an investor. Lei Ju, who was my first angel investor and the chairman of the board of the GWC for three years, and Takeshi Natsuno, who is the chairman of the GWC Japan, are both my mentors.

From today's viewpoint, I think this was the GWC's first story of imagination.

---

[1] This article is a reprint of the speech Wen Chu gave at the GMIC Bangalore 2015.

世界小邮差

2014年我们举办首次GMIC班加罗尔，我问印度合伙人古佩特（Gurpreet Singh）谁是印度最好的移动互联网创新者，我们就邀请他们一起相聚在GMIC班加罗尔！短短两年，Flipkart、Paytm、Olacabs、InMobi、Snapdeal等印度移动互联网行业里最好、最具创新精神的公司创始人和CEO，与我们相聚在这里交流、分享和合作。我相信他们会如中国和硅谷发生的那样，不仅仅是移动互联网行业的创新者，未来也会是印度整个国家引以为自豪的商业领袖。

2014年首次GMIC班加罗尔后，我在印度旅行了27天，从班加罗尔到孟买，从德里到斋浦尔，从鹿野苑到瓦拉那西，我深深叹服这个伟大国家的悠久文化和虔诚的宗教情怀。但我也感受到亟待解决的贫穷问题，无数桥洞里，瘦弱的孩子们那饥饿的眼神，孱弱的母亲翻找垃圾箱中食物的神情让我无法释怀！

我想，GMIC班加罗尔，我们要从中国、从硅谷带来更多的创新思维、创新思想、创新精神，让创新更好地推动印度国家和行业的发展。

我们要和印度的创新者们一起，并做他们的鼓手，传播他们的创新产品与思想，让创新精神更好地在班加罗尔生根发芽，渐渐播撒到印度每一片神奇的土地。

In 2014, we hosted the first GMIC Bangalore. I asked our Indian partner, Mr. Gurpreet Singh, who the most innovative entrepreneurs in India's Mobile Internet industry are. I said, let's invite them all to meet at the conference. In just two short years, the founders and CEOs of Flipkart, Paytm, Olacabs, InMobi, Snapdeal, and many other of the most innovative Mobile Internet companies in India, have attended our conferences to exchange ideas with us. I trust that just like in China and in Silicon Valley, they are not only the best and brightest mind in Mobile Internet, but also the most innovative business leaders of India's future.

In 2014, after the conference, I took 27 days to travel around India, from Bangalore to Mumbai, from Delhi to Jaipur, from Sarnath to Varanasi. I was deeply impressed by this wonderful country's rich culture and devout religious faiths. At the same time, I saw poverty everywhere. I saw starving children look at me with hungry eyes from under bridges, and many mothers, weakened by hunger, searching through trash to find food. I will never forget those scenes.

I believe we can bring innovative thoughts and the spirit of innovation from China and Silicon Valley, in order to help the development of India and its Mobile Internet industry.

I believe we can work hand in hand with India's own innovators, help them promote their innovative products and spread their innovative thoughts, so that the spirit of innovation can truly take root in Bangalore, and from here, spread to every corner of this magical landscape.

世界小邮差

  我们未来商业上的成功是坚守到印度这个国家不再贫穷，妇女孩子不再饥饿的那一天。我和印度团队商量，我们决定捐出本届大会门票收入的一半，给印度本土的一家致力于解决孩子饥饿问题的公益机构。我们知道这份捐赠微乎其微，但我们想从今天开始播种希望！这会是又一次的"想象力"吗？谢谢大家！

文 厨

2015年9月9日

不东 | UNIVERSAL POSTBOY

I believe that our future business success will be realized when the country is no longer impoverished, and its women and children no longer hungry. As such, after consultation with our team in India, we have decided to donate half of the profits of this conference, to an Indian charity organization dedicated to eradicate child hunger. We know that this is only a small donation, but we want to start planting the seeds of hope, starting from today! Will this become another story of imagination? Thank you!

Wen Chu
September 9, 2015

印度"网"事

GMIC班加罗尔召开之际,我在印度工作一周。与前几次在印度到处走走看看不同,这次我基本都在大会举办酒店泰姬珊瑚岛(Vivanta by Taj),坐在酒店花园的那棵数百年的大榕树旁与人聊天,观察大会期间来往宾客,熙攘人群。

大会的热度超过我的预期,参会人数翻番,近5000人,广为印度媒体关注。大会当天及会后,在当地网站、电视和报纸等都有大幅报道。尤其是当一群又一群的印度创业者,挤过来跑过来,激情澎湃,慷慨陈词,"我要做中国的微信""我是中国的大众点评",你会被这股创业热情感染。我仿佛坐着时光机器,穿梭到三五年前的GMIC北京,那时我们还没有搬到国家会议中心办会,也在类似这样的酒店里开始GMIC,此情此景,非常相像。

与几位印度的业界领袖聊,普遍认为三五年后,印度移动互联网会再现中国移动互联网今天的繁荣,他们认为移动互联

不东 | UNIVERSAL POSTBOY

About Mobile Internet in India

Last week, as the GMIC Bangalore was getting underway, I worked in India for a week. Unlike previous visits, when I wandered around, this time I spent most of my time at the Hotel Vivanta by Taj, where the conference was hosted. I sat under the century-old banyan tree in the hotel garden, chatted with friends, and observed the conference attendees and other visitors to the hotel.

The popularity of the conference exceeded my expectation. The number of participants doubled, compared to the previous conference in Bangalore, to nearly 5,000. The conference was also widely covered by Indian media, including newspapers, news websites, and television broadcasts. In particular, groups of Indian entrepreneurs attended the conference with enthusiasm that went through the roof. Some said, I'm going to make an Indian equivalent to WeChat, or to Yelp. Their entrepreneurial spirit was infectious. I felt as if I'd taken a time machine and went back to GMIC Beijing of three or five years ago. At that time, we were still hosting the conference at a hotel like the Vivanta, and had not moved the conference to the China National Convention Center. This scene in India appeared very similar to me.

After chatting with a few industry leaders, we agreed that in three to five years, India's Mobile Internet business would be as prosperous as China's is today.

世界小邮差

网一样是他们祖国的机遇。有印度支付宝之称的Paytm创始人维杰说："我们这群人希望借助移动互联网这股大潮更深远地改变我们这个国家，使之走向强盛。GMIC来印度，意义一样深远。三年前，我就去了GMIC北京，给了我很多启发和帮助，我结识阿里巴巴马云，获得投资（阿里巴巴投资了Paytm近7亿美元），也源于GMIC。GMIC会是传奇！"我说我相信，它会是这个世界的传奇，因为你们就是传奇！维杰15岁中学毕业，打工到创业，自学英语，一步一个脚印，奋斗成功，在印度当地就是一个非常励志的故事。被视为印度亚马逊的电商巨头Flipkart创始人萨钦，也表达了同样的观点：一切移动为先，未来希望Flipkart能帮助数亿印度人更好地享用电商服务，国家变得更好！还要特别说一下，GMIC班加罗尔也是他在印度唯一参加并公开演讲的大会，他每年去GMIC北京都会夫各个会场看看，学习了解和交流，颇有启发。他希望他也能为印度业界做些工作，通过GMIC班加罗尔这个会议平台推动更多从业者参与到移动互联网的大潮中来。

在去机场路上，我发现班加罗尔街道上很少看到纸片了，干净整洁很多，印度总理莫迪正在推动"打扫印度"运动，看来颇有成效！

文 厨

2015年9月17日

不东 | UNIVERSAL POSTBOY

They believed that Mobile Internet represented an opportunity for their country. Vijay Shekhar Sharma, the founder of Paytm, which was known as the AliPay of India, told me that riding on the rise of Mobile Internet, they wanted to transform India and make it a more powerful country. Similarly, it was meaningful for GMIC to come to India. Three years ago, he attended GMIC Beijing, which gave him so much help and inspiration. Through GMIC, he met Jack Ma, and received close to $700 million in funding from Alibaba. He believed that GMIC would become a legend. I told him that I believed the same, that GMIC would become a legend of the world, because of participants like him who were already legends in their own rights. He left school at the age of 15, began to work and subsequently to start his own business. He taught himself English, and achieved what he did today through hard work. He had become a household name and an inspiration in India. Sachin Bansal, the founder of FlipKart, which was known as India's Amazon, expressed similar sentiments. He said that Mobile was his priority, and that in the future, he hoped that Flipkart would be able to help hundreds of millions of Indians to better enjoy e-commerce services, and in the process, make his country a better place. He mentioned specifically that GMIC Bangalore was the only conference he attended and made speeches for in India, and that he went to GMIC Beijing every year to find inspiration and to learn from China's Mobile Internet businesses. He hoped that he would be able to do more for India, and through GMIC Bangalore, promote Mobile Internet and help more entrepreneurs enter the industry.

On the drive to the airport, I realized that the streets of Bangalore were cleaner and had less litter than before. It would seem that Prime Minister Narendra Modi's campaign to "Clean India" was working!

Wen Chu
September 17, 2015

硅谷"网"事

2015年GMIC硅谷期间,滴滴出行的创始人程维、猎豹移动的CEO傅盛来我硅谷的文坊小聚,一起涮火锅。

程维说,这几天在硅谷拜访了些牛人,走访了些公司,感觉硅谷还是居高临下,走在人类最前沿。我看埃隆·马斯克(Elon Musk,特斯拉的创始人),向地球外跨了半步,跟70亿人类就稍显不同。要移民火星,这事人类还没干过,当然他也没干成,但是他先造了火箭,火箭是实实在在上天了,这是路径上的第一步,干成了。所以,我们地球人对火星人仍有期待!

傅盛说,硅谷这儿有印度人、欧洲人、巴西人、墨西哥人,当然还有中国人等,不用较劲你是什么人,想想大家都是地球人就好!

其间,我穿插了一段"网"事,我说我很敬畏的雷军四年前来硅谷,为期一周。在长城会组织的第一天活动上说,他有

不东 | UNIVERSAL POSTBOY

About Mobile Internet in Silicon Valley

During GMIC Silicon Valley, Cheng Wei, the founder of Didi Chuxing, and Fu Sheng, the CEO of Cheetah Mobile, visited my house to have hot pot with me.

Cheng Wei said that they had been visiting top companies and industry leaders in Silicon Valley over the past few days. It would seem that Silicon Valley was still leading the Mobile Internet industry in the world, and was responsible for innovation for all of mankind. Elon Musk, the founder of Tesla, alone out of the seven billion people on earth, already made half a step out of Earth. We had never tried to emigrate to Mars before, of course Musk hadn't either. But still, he produced rockets that really went into space. It was a successful first step. It was not impossible that we should meet Martians soon!

Fu Sheng said that there were Indians, Europeans, Brazilians, Mexicans, Chinese, and many other "shades" of people here in Silicon Valley. No one cared who you were because we were all just Earthlings after all.

I told a story about Lei Jun, the founder of Xiaomi. Four years ago, Lei Jun came to Silicon Valley for a week. He said on the first day of the activities for the

四年没来硅谷了,虽然小米是刚创业,但他有信心小米手机单品卖到100万台;三天后,在一次晚餐会上,他说小米可以销售到1000万台;最后一天在华人聚集的一个沙龙上,他发问式提出,为什么小米不可以全球售出1亿台?如果苹果可以,为什么中国的小米不可以?我至今不清楚,是表达需要还是什么人或事发生了催化作用。由于我全程陪同在听,仔细琢磨,很有感触!

这四年,GMIC硅谷办了四届,也组织G-Trip考察团无数,后来有朋友和会员,决定回国创业的,说创业受到硅谷创业精神的触动;有些说,经营过程中受到硅谷创新思想的启发。

随着GMIC今天的全球八站,长城会未来走向世界的过程中,我们从硅谷受到了什么启示?硅谷在其中发生了什么作用?

聊兴浓烈时,我想起了在自己编辑的"长城会学习机"中看到的一个故事。哥伦布航海,发现了新大陆,就是今天古巴的一个小岛,他决定管理好这个小岛,封了自己做总督,也就是做岛主。但是问题来了,他是一个航海家,一个梦想家,不擅长政治,建立一个有序的治理系统是件巨复杂的事情,而且他面对的还是一群没有文化的"野人",结果可想而知,鸡飞狗跳。后来,他回顾一生,最为他自豪的事情,还是他的四次航海,虽然也有无数凶险,多次海上命悬一线,但探索之行,

GWC, that he had not been to Silicon Valley in four years. He was confident that Xiaomi could sell one million phones. Three days later, at a dinner party, he said that Xiaomi could sell ten million phones. On the last day, at an event for Chinese visitors, he asked, why couldn't Xiaomi sell 100 million? If Apple could do it, why couldn't the Chinese company Xiaomi do the same? To this day, I still had not found out what caused the changes in his estimates, but even so, as I listened to his speech, I became very touched.

In the four years since, GMIC Silicon Valley has hosted four conferences, and also organized G-Trips that brought entrepreneurs from China to visit and learn here. Some members and friends have told me that they were inspired by the entrepreneurial spirit in Silicon Valley and decided to start their own businesses. Some told me that new ideas from Silicon Valley inspired them to operate their businesses differently in some way.

Today, GMIC has eight stops around the world. As the GWC expands globally, what inspiration have we gathered from Silicon Valley? How has Silicon Valley influenced our expansion?

During our conversation, I remembered a story about Christopher Columbus. On his journey, he discovered the New World, an island in today's Cuba. He decided to govern this island, and named himself governor. But the problem was, he was a voyager and a dreamer. He was not good at politics. Establishing a system of rule was a very complicated task. Adding to the problem, his subjects were a bunch of uneducated "savages." You could imagine how badly this venture went. Afterward, when Columbus looked back on his life, what he was most proud of was still his four sea voyages. Even though they were filled with danger, and many times he nearly lost his life, exploration remained his true life's passion.

让其满足而热爱。

发现新大陆，某种意义上是个意外，是上天的馈赠。某种意义上，硅谷的创新对于长城会也是一种馈赠，值得一直探索和追寻。如果我们只有几条船，我们应该探索海洋；如果我们有一支船队，我们应该探索海洋；如果我们有无数船队，我们还是应该探索海洋！

文　厨

2015年10月7日于硅谷半月湾酒店

不东 | UNIVERSAL POSTBOY

Discovering the New World was in some sense a surprise, a present from God. Similarly, innovation in Silicon Valley is a present, one that is worth following and exploring forever. If we have a few ships, we should explore the sea. If we have a fleet, we should explore the sea. If we have countless fleets, we still should explore the sea!

Wen Chu
October 7, 2015

千字文迎郝义

李白斗酒诗百篇,文厨万里千字文。

说起来,我和郝义一起走过的路已经在万里之上。郝义是我们长城会的会员,过去一年多,因为彼此工作的交集,我们在世界各地相会。过去三个多月,因为今天这份合伙人的缘分,我们推杯换盏,指点寰球,把酒言志。

记得我直接从"地球上最著名的中国人之一"聊起,风云际会,盛世中国,峥嵘人生,世界大同。

我们聊到长城会是一幅中国的水墨丹青,也应是世界的油彩工笔;我们聊到长城会从线下到线上,从平面走向立体;我们聊到长城会基于内容,深耕细作,小处着手,大处用心,是创新和人文的交汇、现在与历史的交响。

后来,我们聊到热爱。如果热爱,做地球上最著名的人又

不东 | UNIVERSAL POSTBOY

Welcome E

The poet Li Bai wrote hundreds of poems while drinking. Wen Chu writes articles while traveling tens of thousands of miles.

If one actually tallies the miles E and I have travelled together, the number must exceed tens of thousands of miles. E is a member of the GWC. Over the past year or so, thanks to our various collaborations, we have met in many places across the globe. Over the past three months, we have been meeting up to talk and drink together, in particular to discuss the partnership we are celebrating today.

I remember our conversation started with my goal to become "one of the most famous Chinese people in the world." From there, we went on to discuss the development of China, the rest of the world, life in general, and many other topics of interest.

We agreed that the GWC was like both a traditional Chinese landscape painting, as well as a western-style oil painting. We talked about how the GWC needed to move from offline to online, from two-dimensional to three-dimensional. We said that the GWC was based on content, the details of which we would always pay close attention to, but at the same time, our mission was a great one, it rested at the crossroad between innovation and humanity, between history and modernity.

Later, we talked about passion. With passion, why would I not be able to become

如何？做爱做的事，还能热爱这个世界，人生幸福快乐，莫过于此。

长城会开始"文E组合"新征程，郝义常说，他是一个摇滚歌手，那我就聊做浅吟诗人，我们一起谱写世界的"诗歌"！

文　厨

2015年10月23日

不东 | UNIVERSAL POSTBOY

the most famous person in the world? Doing what I love, and loving this world with passion, these to me were the most joyful things in life.

The GWC is beginning a new journey with this new partnership between Wen and E. Quite frequently, E says that he is like a rock musician. In that case, I am like a wandering bard. Together, we will compose the epic saga of this world!

Wen Chu
October 23, 2015

心意、善意和天意

各位长城会同学，我们同事说，咱们圈内总裁们都在写新年寄语，一则对内鼓舞士气，二则对外传递声音。我想也有道理，辞旧迎新嘛，我就仍以喜欢的方式，作千字文一篇吧。

我看大家对2016年的寄语，有"开心就好"，有"气吞山河"，有"胸怀世界"，有"连接一切"，有"只争第一"，有"大干上市"，有"温暖人心"，等等，都很有意思！正是因为这样，我们这个国家才精彩，才充满希望。我也有三个寄语和大家分享。

心意

心意，就是心里的那份意思。我们办会，还是要用心，认真把工作做好，把心里的那份意思做到。把工作完成，和用心工作，看似一样结果，其实本质不同。郝义同学，上次和大家分享，工作有担责和当责，把工作完成就是担责，也会把结果

不东 | UNIVERSAL POSTBOY

Faith, Kindness, and Providence

Dear GWC Members,

My colleagues have been telling me that all the CEOs we know are writing some New Year felicitations, to give encouragement to the employees and show the public what the company intends to accomplish in the new year. I thought that made sense for this time of year, so I will write one of my articles for the occasion, for the same purpose.

I have read what the others have written. Some said that they wish 2016 to be full of simple happiness, others have great ambitions for what their companies will achieve in the new year. Still others announced that they will take their companies public, or told heartwarming stories. They were all interesting to read. Our nation is interesting because we are all different, and we are all full of hope. I myself have three things to share with you here.

Faith

It is faith in what we do that keeps us going. It is what makes us host conferences with great care, and ensure that our work is done well. Perhaps we could have done the same without this faith, but I don't think it would be the same. Hao Yi said once that work requires responsibility and faith. One could do the job simply

呈现出来，但是比之用心工作的人，我认为的当责者，只是每件小事多做那么一点点，就可以形成无穷的放大效应。用心对我们的会员，他们好多人本身就是我们的朋友，有些还是我们亲密的朋友，我们过去七年的发展，就是源自他们的支持。通过我们的用心工作，把我们的意思传递给他们，他们会感受到的，而且他们都是很有能力有能量的人，他们只要回馈一点点的心意，我们的工作就会越来越顺畅，越来越有力量。用心对我们的客户，他们用钱在对我们的工作，对我们的心意投票。我们的客户越来越多，就是我们彼此心意的互动。要特别关心我们的老客户，我相信这样的道理，只有老客户越来越多，我们的客户工作才是有效的，开个小店讲究回头客，我们办会也一样，而且所有的新客户最终都是老客户！

心意要有，当责方好！

善意

善良比聪明重要。最近这句亚马逊CEO贝索斯（Teff Bezos）的话，微信张小龙又一次强调了。也借此强化微信的底层设计，基本的价值观。我为什么要提及这个呢？2016年开始，我们长城会的GMIC北京要转向公众开放，以前我们只是在国家会议中心办，更多是面向企业，大家都是成年人，都有自己的三观。现在我们同时走向鸟巢办科技盛典，走向奥林匹

because they are responsible for it, but if one believes in the work, no matter how insignificant a job is, then the impact will be great. Our faith makes us treat our members with respect. They are our friends. Some of them are our close friends. The progress we made in the past seven years would not have been possible without their support. We put our soul into our work, so that they could feel our faith. They are also full of energy and positivity themselves. If they return just a little of their own faith, then the work we do will become easier and more meaningful. We put care into our services for our clients, because they are voting for our work and our heart with their money. We will have more clients in the future, and will have exchanges of our mutual faiths. We should take care of our oldest clients in particular, because I believe our ability to retain old clients is a testament to the efficiency of our client service. A small shop relies on its returning customers. We are no different. I hope that all of our new clients will eventually become old clients.

With faith, responsibility will be done just right!

Kindness

Kindness is more important than intelligence. A version of this sentiment was first said by Jeff Bezos from Amazon, and Zhang Xiaolong from WeChat emphasized this again recently in discussing the designs of WeChat and what is deemed valuable by his company. I bring this up now because this year, the GMIC Beijing Conference will be open to the public. Before we hosted our conference at the National Convention Center. We were only facing other businesses. All of the participants were adults with their own morals. But now we are hosting a tech sessions at the Beijing National Stadium and the Olympic Park, which will have close to one million participants from the general public. I believe that there will be parents bringing their children. We will be displaying

克公园办科技庙会，面对的是数十万上百万的人。而且我相信我们的科技庙会还会有很多家长带孩子来参加。我们在展示科技创新，但是大家知道，即使是科技创新，也是有暴力的。甚至有些是科技的暴力美学范畴，可有可无的，这些就需要我们做产品设计时冷静判断，哪怕为了一个孩子，我们就是需要做出取舍。好似我们想得太远了，但这就是"1"，未来所有的"0"都是基于这个"1"！

我们已经在挑战这个世界上最大的科技创新盛会，希望我们2016年开始的时候，能秉承善意，并善待北京这个城市，善待中国这个国家，善待这个世界！有些东西我们必须说不！商业也罢，机会也罢。

天意

天意，就是上天的那份意思。我并不是在搞封建迷信。于我来说，众生意志就是天！沧海桑田就是天！人间正道就是天！

不出数年，文厨就会在中国，我的祖国，或有些国家，拥有俗世的所谓"声名"。我惶恐！我惭愧！我极其感恩！因为长城会真的在干一件了不起的事情！各位长城会同学用心做的善意工作，是令人尊敬的工作，各位长城会会员以及幕后默默支持长城会的那些人，都是极有力量和能量的人！我只因为是

technological innovation, but as everyone knows, technology has the potential to be violent. We have to be careful when we design products then, because if it will affect only one child, then we must make sacrifices accordingly. This will be highly important, and it would be better to be safe than sorry in this matter.

We have set ourselves the challenge of hosting the biggest technology and innovation conference in the world. I hope that we will start the year with kindness: treat the city of Beijing, China, and this world with kindness. We have to say no to some things, no matter how valuable or profitable they might be.

Providence

By providence, I mean the mandate from a higher being. I am not being superstitious because to me, providence means the faith of the masses. It is the passage of time and the moral of the world.

I believe that in a few years' time, my name will be known in China as well as some other countries. I am deeply grateful as well as bashful, because the GWC is doing something incredible. The work of all our members is meaningful, respectable, and full of kindness. The members and those who support the GWC are capable and full of potential. I will be honored only because I founded the GWC, but my honors rightfully belong to every member, every colleague, and every supporter of the GWC.

长城会的第一个人,那个叫创始人的人,很多人心血浇灌的长城会,很多成就与我并不相关,荣耀却转嫁到我的头上!

  这样的事,我也称之为天意。冥冥之中,好似注定;昭昭之行,极为广大。天意如此,我们来干这件事,我们相信移动互联网,我们相信科技,我们相信创新!用我们的方式呈现她,传播她,赞美她!人有心,天有意,是份心意!

文 厨

2016年1月19日

不东 | UNIVERSAL POSTBOY

This is what I consider providence. The GWC is destined for greatness, destined to be well-known across the globe.

Providence has led us to work on this important network. We trust in Mobile Internet, in technology and innovation. We will display it, promote it, and laud it in our own way. If enough people believe in the same thing, then it is great enough to become providence!

Wen Chu
January 19, 2016

交流、交易和交心

亲爱的会员，新年快乐！辞旧迎新之际，常会看到大家公司的总结小视频和年终总结讲话，气吞山河，温暖人心，催人泪下。我也应景附和，作千字文一篇。

交流

每年这个时候，我也会思考，我们长城会如何发展，如何往前走？我就会想到长城会的开始。2008年，樱花3月，我第一次到日本东京，和几位移动互联网的创业者一起，希望与日本行业领先的公司交流学习。我们发现"交流"很困难，原因既有天然的陌生感，也有历史的包袱。今天有所改善，但我仍然发现交流是个永恒的课题！新生儿的第一声哭啼，是交流；游牧农耕、蒸汽火车、电报电话、邮件、微信等都是交流。我相信，无论人类科技文明如何极大丰富，如何叹为观止，人与人都需要交流，也需要面对面的温度感。"见面三分亲！"我是个办会的，我常想，把人聚在一起，会就成了！人的天性就是

不东 | UNIVERSAL POSTBOY

Communication, Transaction, and Connection

Dear Members,

Happy New Year! As we welcome the new year, we often see speeches made by business leaders that conclude the past year and look forward to the future. Some are inspirational, some are heartwarming. I will do the same here with an article of mine.

Communication

Every year around this time, I think about how the GWC will develop going forward, and how we can become even more successful. My mind is always brought back to the beginning of the GWC. It was March in 2008, and I was visiting Tokyo for the first time. Along with a few other Mobile Internet entrepreneurs, I wanted to visit Japanese companies in the industry to learn from them. But what we found was that communication with our Japanese colleagues was very difficult, partly because we did not know each other, and partly because of the difficult history between our countries. This has improved today, but I find that communication is still of the utmost importance to everything we do. Communication includes a baby's first cry and first gesture to his parents; but it also gave rise to farming, steam engines, telegrams and telephones, emails and WeChat. I believe that no matter how advanced technology becomes in the future, we will need communication, we will want the warmth of another human being sitting across from us as we speak. A Chinese saying says, once we meet

需要交流，只是方式不同，力度不同，表现不同。

我们的长城会，仍将把交流这个基本需求作为会员服务的基石。所以我们才会在地球上每个国家和地区举办GMIC，坚持举办各类耗时费神的大小活动，组织大家前往世界各地学习考察。

交易

交易产生价值，交易生发钱财，谈钱不伤感情，还能多合作。交易生长资源，资源优化配置，世界更好。在良好交流的基础上，交易易于进行，我们在会员服务工作中，乐于见到会员之间更多交易，同时我们也乐于见到所有交易能在会员之间直接进行，我们相信"搜完就走"和"用完就走"的价值观，不要有意无意增加介入、截流或各种形式的中间层！

我们有些同事和朋友会提醒，这其中可能错失一些商业利益，我相信正如我尊敬谷歌，"搜完就走"，挣该挣的钱，做该做的事！长城会也一样，而且我有时还隐隐看到长城会的某些独特性，比之谷歌也不逊色。

我们长城会2016年开始，交易的范围会有所扩大，如果我们之前的交易还是在会员们之间进行，从今以后，我们的交易

someone, we are on a friendly footing. Our conferences start by gathering people together. It is a basic human need to communicate. Even if in the future, our mode of communication looks different, the essence will always be the same.

Going forward, this basic need for communication will continue to be the bedrock of the GWC's member services. Communication is the reason that we want to host conferences in every country in the world; the reason that we continue to work on many events, both big and small; and the reason that we have organized trips for our members to study and explore in many places in the world.

Transaction

A transaction creates value and profits, and promote cooperation. It also gives rise to resources, and when those resources are allocated well, then the world becomes a better place. With a firm basis of communication, a transaction becomes easier to carry out, which is why we are happy to see cooperation and transaction between GWC members. We are also happy to see direct transaction between members, because we have enabled them to bypass middlemen and third-parties to build relationships with each other, which is more efficient. We believe in a clean and efficient transaction.

Some of our friends have reminded us that we might miss out on some profits, operating in this manner. But I believe in Google's way of operating, we want to do our jobs well, and make profits where we should. In this area, we are just as efficient as Google, sometimes even more so. I will elaborate on this more in the next point.

Starting this year, the extent of a GWC transaction will be expanded. If before, transactions are conducted between members, then in the future, transactions

也会走向千家万户。2016年全球数十万数百万人会参与到交易的乐趣中来，这也是为什么2016年的GMIC北京，北京国家会议中心、水立方、鸟巢和奥林匹克公园四星连珠，面向数十万大众举办。这也是为什么2016年GMIC全球九站，从特拉维夫到东京，从东京到雅加达，从雅加达到班加罗尔，从班加罗尔到中国台北，从中国台北到硅谷，从硅谷到圣保罗，从圣保罗到首尔……

交心

交心关乎人心，关乎精神，关乎思想！人是感情动物，交流是基本需要，交易是实用的纽带，但心与心的碰撞，精神上的契合，思想上的共鸣，是无与伦比的体验！是穿透空间，甚至是时间的万能钥匙，几乎可以开启一切！

我也试着交交心吧。今天的这篇千字文，我想写给你们，长城会的723名会员。我也没那么重要，虽然我们总是认为自己很重要，其实永远不要低估人性的"居高临下，不喜仰望！"这篇千字文，到底有什么干货呢？充其量不过是插播着小广告的心灵鸡汤，我个人就有一句总结：百无一用是书生，极其无聊是鸡汤。但是我决定写出来，想为你们写，只要有一个人读，我就快乐。

我还年轻的时候，有一次躲在出租屋里写类似的"千字

will be done with the general public. This year alone, nearly one million people will take part in these transactions, which is why this year's GMIC Beijing conferences will be hosted in four locations: the National Convention Center, the Beijing National Stadium, the Olympic Park, and the Water Cube, facing tens of thousands of participants. This is also why we will host GMIC conferences in nine cities across the globe this year, including Tel Aviv, Tokyo, Jakarta, Bangalore, The Chinese Taipei, Silicon Valley, Sau Paulo, and Seoul.

Connection

A connection is an exchange of spirit, thoughts, and feelings. We are emotion-based animals, so communication is a basic human need. Transactions are practical. But a connection in spirt and in thoughts, is an experience like no other. It can even go through time and space. It is the key to everything we do.

Allow me to attempt a connection with you using this article. I don't think that it will be read by very many of you, since you are all very busy. But that isn't important, even though we are accustomed to believe ourselves to be very important. It is always in human nature to want to be superior to others, instead of looking up to others. This article is perhaps not very practical. It is meant to touch the reader, although that is not always relevant. Even so, I wanted to write this to you, because even if only one of you read it, I would be very happy.

In my youth, once I was writing an article like this in my rented apartment, when

文",房东来敲门讨房租,我没敢开门。后来房东终于走了,我折断笔,告诉自己,稿费交不上房租,人生凄凉莫过如此,我今生今世不会再写了。

近来的每篇千字文,我写得好开心!而且我想写就写,不想写就不写!就像我今天想吃盱眙十三香小龙虾就吃盱眙十三香小龙虾,想用盐水煮毛豆就用盐水煮毛豆!

我想写!我想写移动互联网那份精彩,我想写移动互联网那些人!未来有一天,若有机缘,天意如此,我想写这个世界!

我是认真的,交心的!为了未来千字文写得好一点点,我新年还与自己相约,有一个学习探索计划:穿越千年,月新思维和日知录!

"穿越千年"。继在中国台湾地区拜访88岁的诗人余光中体会想象力、拜访89岁的星云大师感受其待人接物"站"着的诚意后,我想在这个世界各地再找到类似的这样八旬以上的十位老人,年龄相加1000年!比如办会的TED创始人美国理查德·沃曼(Richard Wurman)先生,瑞士达沃斯论坛的创始人施瓦布先生,两位都年过八旬,办了一辈子会!我也就是个办会的!我想去请教,去学习,可能的话,我愿接过他们的衣钵,传承和发扬光大他们的办会精神!

the landlord came to ask for the rent. I was scared to open the door, because I didn't have the money. After he finally left, I broke my pencil in half. I told myself that writing was not going to pay for my rent, and that I was not going to write anymore.

But writing these last articles still makes me very happy. I write whenever I want to, just like I eat whatever I want to. There is so much freedom!

I still want to write. I want to record the progress of Mobile Internet, as well as the feats of those involved in the industry. One day in the future, perhaps I will even have the opportunity to write about this world.

I am convicted to making a connection. I made the New Year resolutions to go beyond 1,000 years, renew my thinking every month, and record my life every day.

The idea of "going beyond 1,000 years" came after I visited the 88-year-old Taiwanese poet Yu Guangzhong and the wise 89-year-old monk Hsing Yun, who greeted me with kindness. I decided to find ten other octogenarians like them, whose ages would add up to more than 1,000 years. For example, I plan to visit the founder of TED, Mr. Richard Wurman, and the founder of Swiss Davos, Mr. Klaus Schwab, both of whom are more than 80 years old, and have been hosting conferences all their lives. That is what I do as well, so I want to visit them to learn from them, and in a sense, carry forward their great torches of conference hosting.

世界小邮差

我会去以色列请教94岁的诺贝尔和平奖得主佩雷斯（Shimon Peres）先生，什么是和平；我会去日本请教稻盛和夫先生，什么是"道"，什么是极致，什么是他心目中的日本商道；我会去英国牛津大学待上一阵子，守候霍金先生，问什么是科学、什么是探索、什么是无止境的无知；去梵蒂冈请教方济各教皇，什么是宗教，会让世界和平吗……

"月新思维"。我如此狭隘和自以为是，我需要每月更新思维。2月在美国，沉浸于美国文化中，不拒绝不欢迎，自然而然，说英语过西式生活。3月在以色列，学点希伯来语，融入三大宗教起源地，把自己算作当地人。7月在日本，学着用日语，练书法，学日本人鞠躬。8月，在巴西看奥运会，用葡萄牙语跟人打招呼，去参加里约人的家庭大派对，不会桑巴就扭屁股……

"日知录"，日有所知，晚上记录。或千字文，或寥寥数语，持之以恒。交流、交易和交心！我以"三交"与各位会员相交，长城会以"三交"交天下朋友，长城会"交"出朋友，我们一起珍惜！长城会"交"出生意，我们一起生意盎然！长城会"交"出思想，我们一起呵护！长城会会是传奇！

文 厨

2016年2月4日

不东 | UNIVERSAL POSTBOY

I also plan to visit 94-year-old Israeli Nobel Peace Laureate, Mr. Shimon Peres, and ask him about the meaning of peace. I will go to Japan to visit Mr. Kazuo Inamori, and ask about the meaning of Dao, the Daoist pursuit of the limit, and the Japanese way of business. I will also stay at Oxford University for a while and visit Prof. Stephen Hawking, and learn from him the meaning of science and exploration, and about the great unknown. I will also visit Pope Francis in Rome, and ask about religion, and its ability to achieve world peace.

I am narrow in my thinking, so I need to refresh and renew my thinking every month. I will spend February in the U.S., and immerse myself in American culture. I won't reject or welcome anything forcefully, but simply live an American life and speak English. I will spend March in Israel, learn a little Hebrew, try to assimilate into the birthplace of the three major religions, and live like a local. I will spend July in Japan, speak Japanese and practice calligraphy in Japanese, and learn to bow like a Japanese. I will go to Brazil for the Olympics in August, speak Spanish to the locals, attend family parties in Rio, and make my best attempt at learning samba.

I want to journal every day. Every evening, I will record my daily thoughts in my journal, or write an article. A few paragraphs a day will add up to a large body of work in the long run. Communication, transaction, and connection are what I will use to make friends with our members and everyone else in the world. The GWC will make friends whom we will cherish, make business partners who will flourish with us, and fresh thinking that we will be able to share with everyone. The GWC will become a legend!

Wen Chu
February 4, 2016

世界小邮差

地球上每个人来一次GMIC

亲爱的吉米客：

GMIC的一名大学生志愿者，为每一位参加过GMIC的参会者起了这个特别的名字——吉米客！作为长城会的创始人和联席CEO，这个世界的"小邮差"，我个人很喜欢这个名字。我决定用这个称谓给曾经参加过GMIC的7万多名参会者，写这封特别的邀请信。此时，我正在进行为期一个月的"穿越美国"万里行，自驾车从美国东南角的迈阿密开往西部的加州硅谷，这也是我人生中最长的一次旅行！

我就从本次旅行开始的迈阿密写起，我首先去拜会了一位办会的前辈，TED创始人理查德·沃曼。我带着"地球上每个人来一次GMIC"的梦想去请教他，他鼓励我追逐自己内心的渴望，追逐自己的好奇心。即使办一辈子的会，也要办不一样的会！我需要"Care nothing""No education, only learning！"

不东 | UNIVERSAL POSTBOY

Everyone Comes to GMIC

Dear GMICers,

One of GMIC volunteers came up with this wonderful name for everyone who has ever participated in a GMIC—GMICer (pronounced Gee-Meeker)! As the founder and co-CEO, as well as the "Universal Postboy", I personally love this name, which is why I am addressing this letter to the 70,000 people who have attended in a conference in this way. I am currently on a month-long journey across the U.S., driving from Miami in the southeastern corner, to Silicon Valley in the west, my longest journey ever!

I'll write about Miami first, where I started my drive. In Miami, I visited Richard Wurman, the founder of TED and my senior in hosting conferences. I told him about my dream of "Everyone comes to GMIC." He encouraged me to follow my passion and curiosity. I can do nothing except hosting conferences all my life, and still manage to achieve bigger and better dreams with this single task. He advised me to "care nothing" and to believe in "No education, only learning."

其次，我来到了奥兰多的迪士尼。我刚刚懂事的女儿也是第一次到迪士尼，她说："I am happy, I am very happy!"（我很快乐，非常快乐！）我得到一个小的启示：快乐！过去七年，GMIC主要是面向企业，面向各位高大上的移动互联网精英，面向移动互联网企业。2016年，GMIC将走向大众，走到千家万户，面向各行各业，甚至面向我们未来的可爱的孩子们！GMIC北京将首次在中国国家体育馆鸟巢举办"科技庙会"，我们将面向数十万人，呈现科技的乐趣、创新的魅力。不仅仅是那些成年人，包括我们可爱的孩子们。我有一个梦想：GMIC科技庙会有一天被孩子们视为在这个科技创新时代又一个"迪士尼乐园"。

在肯尼迪航空航天中心，我赞叹人类充满无尽想象的"探索"历程。2016年，GMIC全球九站将携手这些卓越的探索者，把探索的精神植根于每位吉米客的心中。

华盛顿，这个强调自由民主的美国首都，我感受最深的是她的"开放"。没有围墙的白宫，自由进出的总统府，免费的博物馆，等等，无处不彰显着开放的气息。GMIC要开放。我有一个梦想：有一天，GMIC遍布地球上的每一个国家和每一个地区！

从芝加哥，我踏上了美国的"母亲之路"，传奇的美国66号公路。一座座二十世纪早期的博物馆、彩色沙漠（Painted

My second stop was Disney World in Orlando. This was the first time my daughter had been to Disney. She said, "I am happy, I am very happy!" I took that as inspiration to be happy myself. Over the past seven years, GMIC's primary audience was other businesses. We were serving elites and top talents of the Mobile Internet industry. 2016, GMIC will be open to the public, to the masses. Our participants will come from every industry, and will include children, who are our future. We will showcase the joy to be found in technology and innovation to tens of thousands of participants at our tech conferences at the Olympic Park and the National Stadium. My dream includes children as well as adults. I hope that one day, kids can view GMIC tech conference as another Disney World in the age of technological innovation.

At the Kennedy Space Center, I was amazed by mankind's limitless imagination and exploration. 2016, the nine stops of GMIC around the world will work with these explorers, to plant the spirit of exploration in the heart of every GMICer.

In Washington D.C., the capital of this country that believes in democracy above all else, my deepest impression was of its openness. The White House was not enclosed by walls; the governor's mansion could be entered at will; and the museums did not charge an entrance fee. It was open everywhere. GMIC should be open as well. I have a dream that one day, GMIC will be hosted in every country and region in the world.

From Chicago, I embarked on the "Mother Road", the legendary U.S. Route 66. I saw museums from the early 20th century, painted deserts, and the Grand

Desert)、大峡谷(Grand Canyon),等等,这是美国梦开始的地方。今天我的祖国也提出了"中国梦",我也想起了中国的"丝绸之路"。我有一个梦想:有一天,不管是美国梦还是中国梦,世界上的每个国家都有自己的梦,GMIC将融入每个国家梦。GMIC全球各站就像美国66号公路,就像"丝绸之路",是连接每个国家的"移动互联网之路""科技创新之路"。

好莱坞,GMIC需要有"好莱坞",我们正在进行科技遇上娱乐,移动互联网遇上音乐,你中有我,我中有你。这个世界因为"娱乐"更美好!

硅谷,过去三年,这个"创新"的圣地是我停留最多的地方!从我创立长城会的第一天开始,我把自己视为地球人。我今天仍以一名中国人而自豪,硅谷这块神奇的土地赐予我无尽的能量,我吸收了无尽的灵感。我有一个梦想:有一天,GMIC能有幸成为一名创新的使者,把创新的精神播撒到世界各地!

再次出发,再次出发,再次出发!7万吉米客,距离地球上70亿人类,中间相差几个零。2016年我们会有70万吉米客,相聚GMIC全球各站。跟随魅力十足的时间隧道,有一天,我们会有700万吉米客;有一天,地球上只有两类人,吉米客和非吉米客;有一天,地球上人人都是吉米客!

不东 | UNIVERSAL POSTBOY

Canyon, where the American Dream started. China has come up with the "Chinese Dream", which reminds me of the Silk Road. I have a dream that one day, every country will have its own dream, and GMIC will be a part of all those dreams. Just like Route 66 and the Silk Road, GMIC will connect Mobile Internet networks and the paths to technology and innovation in every country.

Hollywood should figure in GMIC, where technology meets entertainment, and Mobile Internet meets music. All of these industries should be interconnected. The world has become a better place because it has been greatly entertained.

Over the past three years, I have lived in Silicon Valley, this mecca of innovation, longer than anywhere else. I began to view myself more as an "Earthling" the day I founded the GWC. Today I am still proud to be Chinese, it is Silicon Valley that has gifted me with boundless energy and limitless inspiration. I have a dream that one day, GMIC will be lucky enough to be a messenger of innovation, and spread the spirit of innovation around the world.

Beginning again! Beginning again! Beginning again! There are 70,000 GMICers currently, a few zeros away from the seven billion people on earth. In 2016, 700,000 GMICers will gather at our conferences around the world. In time, we will have seven million; and one day, the world will only have two kinds of people, GMICers and non-GMICer; eventually, everyone will be a GMICer!

世界小邮差

最后，我想起了Facebook、微信和Line（连我），地球上已经有在网上建立起来的数亿甚至数十亿人的连接，这些连接是在"天上云里"。今天，我们用GMIC来连接，让我们回到地上和人与人之间的温度里！我们要共同过"天上和人间"连接起来的美好生活！以上三家公司的创始人就是吉米客！我们是吉米客！我们的朋友会是吉米客吗？我们的同事会是吉米客吗？我们的客户会是吉米客吗？我们的朋友的同事会是吉米客吗？我们的同事的客户会是吉米客吗？我们的朋友的同事的客户会是吉米客吗？

我有一个梦想，"会"的开始；我们有一个梦想，那一定会！

文　厨

2016年3月9日

不东 | UNIVERSAL POSTBOY

Finally, I think about Facebook, WeChat, and Line. Already, billions have been connected through the Internet, connections made online and in the "cloud." Today, we are connecting through GMIC in traditional face-to-face connections. One day, our lives will be connected both online and in-person. The founders of all three companies--Facebook, WeChat, and Line, are already GMICers. We are GMICers. Will our friends and colleagues become GMICers? How about our clients, our friends' colleagues, or the clients of our friends' colleagues?

I have a dream, a dream of possibilities: because if we have a dream, it will be realized!

Wen Chu
March 9, 2016

日久之道[①]

我是长城会创始人和联席CEO，我刚在演讲前的最后一分钟还在准备我今天的发言，我希望能够把最新的一些情况给大家做一个分享。

我今天分享的主题就一个字——"久"。

这一次我们来到日本，除了办GMIC东京，还有一个高山探索（GASA Exploring）的行程。大家跟我一起在一周的时间里，拜访一些日本企业界和文化界的人，跟我一起去的包括我们今天见到的演讲者，包括百度的总裁张亚勤、猎豹移动的傅盛、易到用车的周航、经纬创投的张颖，等等，都是我们中国业界著名的创业者和企业家。

在为期一周的过程当中，我还是得到了一些启发，我就想把

[①] 本文是GMIC2015班加罗尔站的演讲稿。

不东 | UNIVERSAL POSTBOY

The Long-Lasting Way[1]

I am the founder and co-CEO of the GWC. I was preparing this speech until the last second today, because I wanted to share the latest news with you all.

My theme today is a single word: long-lasting.

This time we came to Japan, in addition to hosting GMIC Tokyo, we also organized an exploratory trip called "GASA Exploring." In a week's time, the participants and I visited well-known people in the business and cultural sectors of Japan. Some of our speakers today, including Zhang Yaqin, the CEO of Baidu, Fu Sheng of Cheetah Mobile, Zhou Hang of Yongche, Zhang Yin of Matrix Partners, and many other well-known entrepreneurs and business leaders were with me.

I found great inspiration during that week, which is what I will share with you

---

[1] This was the speech I made at the GMIC Tokyo 2016.

这些启发做一些分享，准备得不是太充分，但是每一个思考都是我最新的思考，所以我把今天的主题定为"久"。同样我用几个字来解读、分享一下，我怎么理解这一次的日本考察行程。

第一个字是"素"，朴素的素。

这个字是我从无印良品的CEO松崎晓那边得到的，他在介绍无印良品的品牌理念和经营理念的时候强调"素"这个字，叫"简素"。具体来讲，因为很多词很难非常精确地说出来，但是大概的意思是"简约"，"素"代表了"简约"。他说无印良品在品牌经营的过程当中，逐渐回归到简约，他认为"简约""有用"是品牌核心的理念。

第二个字，叫作"空"。

这个字是无印良品首席设计师原研哉先生提出的，他在我们三个小时的拜访过程中，给我们系统分享了他怎么去解读当前无印良品的品牌理念。他认为简约和简洁这个"素"，到今天为止他逐渐在里面有一个思考，就是"空"。我们就问他，到底"素"和"空"怎么理解呢？某种意义上都是简洁的意思，很多事情是只可意会不可言传的。后来他大概用了至少半个小时解读，什么叫"简约"，什么叫"素"，什么叫"空"，以及三者的区别。坦白告诉大家，半个小时以后，我

不东 | UNIVERSAL POSTBOY

today. I am not perfectly prepared, but everything I will talk about represents my latest thinking. I will talk about "long-lasting", and will explain this single word to you with the help of a few other words, as well as drawing on my experience from that trip to Japan.

The first word is "unadorned."

I learned this word from the CEO of Muji, Mr. Satoru Matsuzaki, when he introduced the company's branding and operational concepts to me. More specifically, "unadorned" stood for simplicity in design and in the way Muji operated. He said that Muji slowly returned to simplicity, because he believed that simple but utilitarian products were at the core of the brand's value.

The second word is "bare."

This word came from the lead designer of Muji, Mr. Kenya Hara. We visited him for three hours, during which he systematically shared with us how he understood Muji's current brand concept. "Bare" arose gradually out of his meditation on "unadorned." We asked him, how we could understand the two concepts as they related to each other. In some sense, both meant simplicity. He spoke for at least half an hour on simplicity, and on the difference between "unadorned" and "bare." But to be frank, I still don't completely understand these two difficult to differentiate concepts afterward.

还是听得不是很明白，因为这个观点本来很难讲。

但是有一点很有意思，他说，你看，"简约"的构成是和以前做对比得来的，比如唐朝的时候，皇宫里面的东西都是很复杂的，所有金碧辉煌的建筑、金碧辉煌的器皿，然后这些东西不断被简单化，就显得越来越简洁。简洁同样还是会有两种感觉和状态，有些东西，我印象很深，我一直很想调出那张图，他用了两把小刀（举例），一个是大拇指摁住的刀柄，他说你看这个很简约的，但是还是需要大拇指按住，方便使用，这可以看成"简约""素"。

那么什么叫"空"呢？就是只有一个刀柄和刀，这个时候你想怎么用都行，你拇指怎么按都行，这个相当于"空"。即使是这样讲，在他当时表达的时候，我脑海里想到一首诗："千山鸟飞绝，万径人踪灭。孤舟蓑笠翁，独钓寒江雪。"那种画面感就呈现在我脑海里。其实你很难说清楚唐诗表明的状态。同样后来我又倒推，什么是"素"呢？非常简单的，有一首著名的诗，骆宾王写的"白毛浮绿水，红掌拨清波"，好像非常简单，读起来像是小朋友写的诗，那时候他还很小，很有意思。这是我想到的第二个字，就是"空"。

还有第三个字——"枯"。

不东 | UNIVERSAL POSTBOY

But one of his points did stay with me. He told me that "simplicity" represented a comparison with the past. If one looked at a Tang Dynasty palace, one would see that everything was adorned in a complicated way. The buildings were decorated in gold, and the furnishing was trimmed in gold as well. But after that, everything began to be simplified, so that it became cleaner and simpler in design. I remember one photo he showed us that stayed with me long after. He used two knives as an example. One of the knives could only be used when he pressed his thumb against the handle. He said that even though the design of the knife was simple, it still had to be used in the right way. This was the meaning of "unadorned" and "simple."

What then was "bare"? The other knife was a simpler one with a handle, and you could use it however you wanted, and put your thumb wherever you wanted, this was "bare." As he explained, a Chinese poem came to my mind that roughly translates to: "The birds have left these mountains, and people have vacated the mountain paths. Only a single boat with a lone fisherman remains, fishing on the snow-covered river." That was my mental image. Poems often create an atmosphere like this that is difficult to explain otherwise. Later on, I thought in the same way about the meaning of "unadorned", and similarly, a poem came to mind, one that we all know well. Luo Binwang wrote about geese swimming, and described them as "white feathers floating on green water, while red feet paddled the clear waves." The poem sounds simple enough, as if written by a child. In fact, the poet was quite young when he wrote this poem. This was what I thought of when I meditated on "unadorned."

The third word is "wither."

The famous Japanese garden designer, Shunmyō Masuno, visited us today. I interviewed him. Yesterday, we visited his temple and talked with him for more

今天我们的枯山水大师枡野俊明也来了，我也跟他做了访谈。昨天我们还去了他的寺庙，聊了大概有两个多小时。今天在论坛上我还问了他，到底什么是"枯"。他今天又做了阐述，就是你慢慢减少减少，减少到一定时候就是"简约"，这个简约就是他呈现在山水设计上的"枯"的概念，你没有山水，只是营造的意境，这是他想表达的，这个词使我想到了"枯"。

我还想到了一个字——"专"。

这个是从哪个企业家那儿来的呢？是FANUC（发那科）创始人讲了一个故事，他说："我们已经是机械机器人领域里最大的公司了，但是我们认为，在接下来很长一段时间，我们还是会专心致志做好机械方面的机器人，不会因为人工智能很火就做人工智能。我们可能用人工智能的东西做研究和分析，但我们现在还是专心致志地聚焦在怎么做好机械机器人。"这是我学到的第四个字。

第五个字——"顺"。

我们最近也拜访了一家公司，这家公司快两百年了，叫古河电工。他们公司的CEO跟我们说，持续经营两百年的原因是顺应时代的潮流。我以前认为做得久的企业和组织，一般来说是"软"的东西，虚的东西，不是实的东西。大家知道古河电

than two hours. At the forum today, I asked him about the meaning of "wither." He explained that wither meant a gradual lessening, lessening to the point of "simplicity." This was his approach to designing gardens as well. An atmosphere could be created in the garden in the absence of the usual adornments, like rocks or streams. This I believe is the meaning of "wither."

I have also thought of another word—"dedication."

This word came from a story told by the founder of FANUC. He said that they were already the biggest company in robotics, but they believed that for a very long time in the future, they would still be dedicated to making the best robots. They would not venture into Artificial Intelligence just because that became popular. They might put some effort into researching and analyzing AI-related data, but their dedication was to make the best robots. So "dedication" was the fourth word I learned.

The fifth word means "Going Along."

We recently visited a company, Furukawa Electric, that had been in business for nearly 200 years. The CEO of the company told us that they had thrived for 200 years because they understood and had always gone along with the current of the time. I used to think that companies that had been in business for a long time would not be in the business of producing physical things, but in fact, Furukawa manufactures fiber optic cables, plastic, and many other definitively physical

工是做光缆、光纤，以及塑料的企业，属于实的东西。当时我把观点抛给他，说比较传统的东西，像大学、寺庙、宗教，等等这些常见的，都没有什么实体。

他表达了一个很有意思的观点，"我们是做金属的，我们所有的东西都是金属的，从一开始做铜制品起家，做光纤，做新材料，包括现在做最前沿的复合材料，等等，都可以看作金属制品。我们认为做金属制品，只要认真做，专注，把它做到极致，顺应时代潮流，一样可以做得很久"。这很启发我，我以前片面地认为，一些"软"的虚的东西更容易久，其实金属是最实的东西了，只要顺应时代的潮流，做到极致，其实也可以做成两百年的公司。

这些是我这次在日本六天行程当中，拜访日本的企业、文化界的大师给我的一些启发，我分享出来，就是这五个字。

最后，我回到我们的主题，就是"久"。

我非常感慨地在思考一个问题，就是长城会有没有机会成为一家千年组织？

如果不是来到日本，我真心不敢想这个事情。你看，日本百年老店很多，在我们中国，三十年、五十年的公司和品牌已

products. I asked the CEO about this, and wondered if it wouldn't be easier for more traditional organizations, like universities, temples, and other religious places, to thrive on ideas or practices, theoretical things instead of physical products.

He expressed an interesting view in response. He said that they were in the metal business, so they manufactured all of their products using metal. At first, they dealt with copper, making fiber optic cables and many composite metal products. They saw it as their mission to always make metal as best as they could, but in a way that went along with the trends of the time. In this way, the company was able to stay in business for a very long time. This inspired me and opened my eyes to possibilities, because I used to think non-physical businesses were more long-lasting, but metal was as physical and concrete as it got. So, as long as a company does what it does as best as it can, in a way that fits in with the time it is in, then it can thrive for hundreds of years.

These are the five words that I learned from my six-day trip to Japan, where I visited Japanese businesses and cultural giants, and was inspired by them.

Now, let us return to our theme, "long-lasting."

I became a little emotional thinking about a question: could the GWC become a thousand-year-old organization?

I would never have dared to dream of that, had I not been to Japan. There were stores in Japan that had been operating for hundreds of years, whereas in China, it would be rare to find a company or a brand that had survived beyond 30 or 50 years. I was especially touched when we visited Fujitsu, which came much

世界小邮差

经很难得了,但是在日本一百年的有很多。令我很震撼的一件事情就是富士通,它属于古河电工的孙子辈的公司,可能还是重孙子辈的公司,反正晚了很多年了。我们这些创始人都说,我觉得你们企业历史很久了,富士通也是五六十年了,他们马上就非常谦虚地、不好意思地说,我们企业历史还是很短的,在日本很多企业确实非常长久。

我回归到长城会这个事情,做这个会议,做交流,所以要"久"。最后,我很高兴来到日本,也很感谢大家支持GMIC东京,我们希望能够长长久久地把GMIC在日本、在东京做下去,希望越久越好。我们也会思考,怎么样让长城会继续长长久久地做下去,成为一个千年组织,我想这里面一定会非常有意思的。谢谢大家!

文 厨
2016年7月16日于东京

不东 | UNIVERSAL POSTBOY

later than companies like Furukawa. Fujitsu had been in business for more than 50 years. When we visited, we were impressed by its long-time success, but the people at Fujitsu told us humbly that they had not been around for very long, especially compared to many other Japanese companies.

Let us return to the GWC. A conference is meant to serve as an opportunity for exchanges, which is precisely why it needs to last for a long time. Lastly, I am grateful to be in Japan, and I want to thank everyone for your support for GMIC Tokyo. We hope that GMIC will last for a long time in Japan, in Tokyo, and become better and better. We will think long and hard about how to allow the GWC to last for a long time, to become a thousand-year-old organization. I trust that it will be an interesting and fulfilling journey. Thank you!

Wen Chu
July 16, 2016

搭手

最近在硅谷，每天跟英语老师学习两个小时英语，不知不觉近一个月，居然感觉到有些进步了。记得起初我和英语老师商量，这次打算在美国停留100天，想充分利用这100天好好补补英语，能不能请老师每天来我的办公室，这样我可以工作和学习两不误。这是很奢侈的想法，老师是斯坦福语言教学方面的名师，平时有很多学生，教学任务很重，但是她真的挤出了时间，每天准时来悉心教导我，每节课都认真地针对我的实际情况和不足之处进行备课，用心地引导我。我自己都觉得不可思议，为什么她如此投入和用心？有一次，课间聊天，她动情地对我说："你会是我这一生最得意的学生，我教授了几十年的学生，有很多英文基础比你好的，也有不如你的，但是，我想教会你英语，教会你英语，这个世界上很多人将来都会因此受益！"我感动得无以言表，只有认真去学。今天这样的机缘我称之为"搭手"，我这一生真的何其幸运，竟有如此多的老师、长者、朋友、伙伴和亲人"搭手"！

不东 | UNIVERSAL POSTBOY

八年前,我的第一个天使投资人雷军,手把手教我创业,我尊之为老师。我在日本的第一个投资人夏野刚,是我心目中地球上最幽默的老师,七年前,他指着一桌子日本数一数二的创业界的新锐说,你们不要小看这位年轻人,他冒冒失失地来找我,说要来帮助两国移动互联网行业交流合作,对两国人民的友谊也有意义,我被他的真诚打动,虽然他是一个中国人,我心里很想他是一个日本人,但我决定帮助他!两年前,我多次拜访诗人余光中,长者为我解开了对想象力的恐惧感的纠结,他说伟大的政治家丘吉尔就是一个很有想象力的人,那你为什么对你的一些所谓的"胡思乱想"要感到恐惧呢?2016年,我连续几次受教于TED创始人理查德·沃曼,老人家提醒我,你可以一辈子办会,但是一定要办不一样的会!追逐你的好奇心,追逐你的渴望,无所畏惧,一往无前。两个月前,霍金教授为GMIC站台,为"科学复兴"呼吁,一句"New Scientific Renaissance"如有魔力,使亿万人共振奋。

但内心极度"自负"之小我,在感激"搭手"之恩的同时,每每自问,我如何方能如他们一样甚至超越他们?我如何不辜负这份"搭手"的机缘,更深远地影响和惠及这个世界?

近来,我把目光也投向中华文明五千年来的那些智者:公元629—645年西行求法的唐玄奘,公元前139年出使西域的汉张骞……。我和太太说,这次我会在美国待100天,并尽量待在硅谷，在家里多陪陪你和孩子们。太太很惊讶。近两年，我几乎没有在家超过一个月的情况，或工作出差，或周游列国。我说，这100天之后，我想"搭手"汉唐盛世之张骞、玄奘，当然也再请老板你"搭个手"，去进行100个国家的"科学复兴"之路，比丝绸之路、西天取经之路甚至我们祖国的"一带一路"，要走得更远。

我也诚恳地告诉我的创业伙伴和同事们，我这一生还是会毫无悬念地成为一个"亿万富翁"，但我志不在此，我向往一千年前的一个叫李白的人，洒脱！我这辈子诗词文章没有可能像他那样了，但我向往他的洒脱，以后大块吃肉大把数钱主要拜托大家了！

我也常常对长城会会员和我亲密的朋友们倾诉衷肠，我很喜欢两千多年前的史学家司马迁，深邃！对人心的洞察令人叹为观止！我一直认为，我哪里是个能够做好服务的创始人？你我相知相识，大多交流交易，何时可以交心？

2016年以来，办GASA大学，作为第一位报名的学生，我想起公元前551年的孔子，还有我喜欢的孟子，前五百年后五百年，舍我其谁？

"搭手"。我尝试搭他们的手，这些前辈，我无意间发现他们影响了我，无意间他们似乎也在为我"搭手"……

"搭手"于我而言，已经不仅仅是心存感激，不仅仅是榜样和超越，不仅仅是世俗的峥嵘，某种意义上，我归之为，一切都是天意！

文　厨

2017年6月4日独酌半斤或八两随笔于硅谷文坊

会　神

聚精会神，这个成语的意思是指集中注意力的样子，引申指专心致志。我今天用这个词，有两重意思，一个是指聚精会神地办会，一个是办会入神。

有一个很有趣的现象，各行各业好像都有各方"神""圣"，商业有商业上的神，艺术有艺术上的神。比如说日本有经营四圣：稻盛和夫、盛田昭夫、本田宗一郎、松下幸之助。一个寿司店，经营了数十年之后，就出现了寿司之神。我还有幸去拜访这个被称为寿司之神的小野二郎，心怀敬仰地吃了一次他亲手制作的寿司大餐。日本有一个存在千年的花道圣地池坊，就在京都的六角楼。其中有位在日本被称为花道之神的人物，就连日本著名的政治家丰臣秀吉也非常敬慕他。此外，琴棋书画，琴有琴圣，围棋有无数棋圣，书圣王羲之，画圣顾恺之。茶道也有茶圣，就是写《茶经》的陆羽。总之，各种神各种圣，各种神圣，好像没听说过有会神、会圣，会虫倒是常常听人提起。

那么有没有可能出现办会办到极致,而出神入圣呢?对此的思考,颇有点入神了。聚精会神地想了想,这十年来我确实认认真真地办了一些会,也曾经总结了一系列的方法论。比如说大"展"宏图,如果一个会能够把展做大,那么会就扎实。美国的CES(国际消费类电子产品展览会)就是大展宏图。比如说,大会无形,我去美国的西南偏南音乐展会,这个会开在奥斯汀城市的每一个角落——河边的码头、Live House(小型现场演出的场所),甚至是大马路的中间。原来大会是可以如音乐一样弥漫在城市的每个角落,而不仅仅是聚集在所谓大型会议场所和展厅。此外,选择在正确的时间、正确的地点办正确的会,要天时地利人和,等等。但是,即使无比正确,大展宏图的CES、大会无形的西南偏南,也都占了天时地利人和,谈不上办会者到了出神入圣的境界。

我想起了81岁高龄的TED创始人理查德·沃曼第一次见面时和我说的第一句话:你可以一辈子办会,但一定要办不一样的会!那么到底什么是不一样的会呢?CES、西南偏南,甚至是大到奥运会、世博会,高到达沃斯,似乎都没有做到真正的极致。或许所有高、大的会才是成功的,这一看法可能本身就是一个误解。换个角度想想,这个世界上的万事万物哪一样不是会呢?我们GMIC大会固然是科技互联网大会;长城会的饭局也是会;全球商务考察,深入到每一个企业,是交流合作会;GMIC X科技奥斯卡,会在奖中,奖在会中;GASA大学,和科学家交朋友，邀请最有潜质改变世界的一群人，一起探索科学思维、视野和思想，是探索科学精神的"会"……

人生无处不是"会"，处处留心可入"神"！

不知道从什么时候开始，我自己就相信了"会"不是一个好的商业模式。似乎办会的前辈们，都没有所谓世俗的商业上的极大成功。这是不是也是一种偏见呢？

我又一次想到了常常在"会"中运用的想象力。过去这两年，我很享受想象力的美妙，以办会为名，见科技大咖、见明星艺人、见思想长者、见科学大家。如今在探索见各城市市长、列国首脑，等等，似乎也只见了冰山一角。就比如世俗的名利吧，名利名利，我既无约定俗成之实名，也无从容不迫之实利。名为大器，自有天成，而在其后的利，于我来说，一直都视为末技，但末技也未上手，怎么到现在我也没能完成赚上一个亿的"小目标"呢？就运用想象力探索，科学复兴就是想象力！科学复兴现在加上这个维度，顺势完成"小目标"一个亿，时间一年为限。逆向想象，长城会也是独角兽的规模，我个人至少也能赚上一个亿。如果长城会自身做不到，基于长城会平台的延展，我也会展开商业想象的翅膀。

会，不是人云亦云的会。以上的一切，皆为过往，都是探索。在我心中，人情冷暖，喜怒哀乐，见天地见众生见自己，繁体的"會"字，天、地、人尽在其中。

No education, only learning! （没有受教，求知探索）

文　厨
2017年感恩节之夜于硅谷

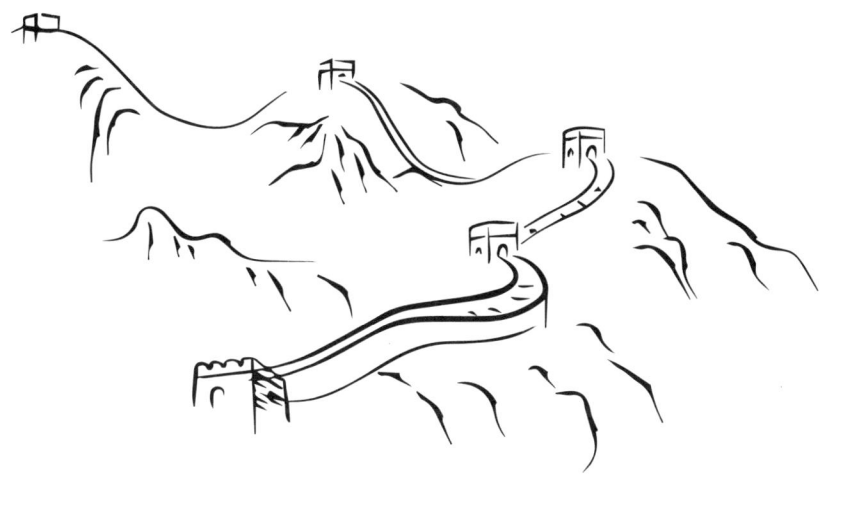

「见」

"问"诗人余光中

余光中,台湾著名诗人(1928—2017年)。2015年在他高雄的家中,我们聊了三个小时。

话题从我介绍"长城会学习机"开始。这几年,行走世界,深感世界如此不同,文化多元,山川秀丽,人物峥嵘。为了学习和了解这个世界,我给自己编辑了一部学习机,其实就是一台最大存储容量的iPad,其中内容是我收集的认为有价值的人物影像、音乐、图片、文字等,而且我每个国家和地区只选择一个代表,我想尽量了解这个星球上多些国家和地区,即使我只了解一个国家和地区的一个人,也要了解将近200个人,已经是很大的工作量。

比如美国,我只选择了"我有一个梦想"的马丁·路德·金,忍痛放弃了被称为美国最伟大的总统林肯,也放弃了那位讨人喜欢的骨子里就幽默的马克·吐温,虽然我骨子里是个一点都不幽默的人,但不影响我对他的喜爱;印度我选择了

不东 | UNIVERSAL POSTBOY

"Asking" The Poet Yu Guangzhong

Yu Guangzhong is a very well-known poet from Taiwan Area. He is 88 years old. We talked for three hours in his home in Kaohsiung, Taiwan.

We started with my GWC "Learning Machine." In recent years, I have been traveling around the world, and have been stunned by how different every country is in terms of their cultures, vistas, and their people. In order to learn about the world, I made myself a "Learning Machine"—an iPad with the biggest possible storage space, in which I have collected the most valuable content about the most important people. I have only selected one person as the representative for each country, because I want to learn about all the countries. If I only learn about one person per country, that is still nearly 200 people, which is quite a lot of work.

For example, I chose Martin Luther King, and gave up President Lincoln, who I believe is the greatest American president, as well as the humorous and likeable Mark Twain. Even though I am not funny at all myself, I can still appreciate Mr. Twain. I chose Mahatma Gandhi for India, for his perseverance and self-

甘地，感叹他的坚韧和艰苦卓绝的自省自律以及"非暴力不合作运动"，将毕生心血奉献给印度民主和独立；西班牙是哥伦布，发现新大陆的意义，胜过拿破仑的百万雄狮和成吉思汗横扫欧亚大陆的金戈铁马；意大利是马可·波罗，传奇的旅行家；俄国是作家列夫·托尔斯泰，勿以暴力抗恶；日本是宫崎骏，唯美梦幻的漫画世界；牙买加的鲍勃·马利，世界和平主义的音乐人；等等，我认为这些人是他们各自国家的也是这个世界的梦想者（visionaries）。我用这个学习机一边学习英语，一边了解这个丰富多彩的世界。我也希望通过学习机让长城会会员们多些了解这个多元的世界，体会不同的文化和不同的人生。

诗人说，这个就是"想象力"。你也可以把你说的这些梦想者看成是远见者（seer），能比较现在的事件、过去的历史并放眼未来。或者说是先知——那些先知先觉者，有预知未来能力的人。

诗人说，你是移动互联网的，但我没有手机，不上网，不打电话，不发信息。想象力会帮助我们，我们能跟上帝沟通，你去教堂祷告，是对上帝说，但有人说，从未听到过回话。怎么没有呢？你看天上的闪电！

诗人说，想象力不仅对于文学创作非常重要，对于大思

reflection, as well as his "satyagraha movement" and his dedication for India's democracy and independence. Christopher Columbus represents Spain, whose discovery of the New World outweighs Napoleon and Genghis Khan's armies. For Italy, I chose Marco Polo, legendary traveler to Asia. For Russia, I chose Leo Tolstoy; for Japan, Hayao Miyazaki and his dreamy animated world; Jamaica, Bob Marley, a musician for world peace; and many others. I believe these people are visionaries of their nations as well as the world. I am using this "Learning Machine" to learn English while I get to know this wonderful world. I hope that it will help the GWC members to get to know the world as well, with its different cultures and unique lives.

The poet said that this was "imagination". You could also call these visionaries "seers", because they could hold history, current events, and the future side by side and compare them. Or you could call them prophets, because in some sense, they had the ability to predict the future.

He also said, you work in the Mobile Internet industry. By comparison, I do not even have a cell phone, use the Internet, make calls or send text messages. Imagination helps us to communicate with God. You could pray in church and speak with God. One might ask, how come I have never received a response? Have you not? Look at the lightning in the sky.

He said that imagination is not only important to creative writing, but important also for philosophers, thinkers, artists, as well as politicians. For example, Vincent

想家、哲学家、艺术家包括政治家也非常重要。比如我喜爱的梵高，生前画作一文不值，死后却件件价值连城，我们后人就是在感受他的惊人的想象力。丘吉尔在第二次世界大战时挺身而出；战后参加竞选失败，收拾包裹就回家，一声不吭，不闹腾，这就是伟大的政治家。孙中山也是先知，预见了晚清的覆灭，政治潮流的浩浩荡荡。

谈话期间，诗人言辞智慧，妙语连珠。

诗人说，我跟你们搞网络的人合作较少，我几年前参加过一次大哥大电信公司的短信征文比赛，至今还能记得一些获奖短信。"父亲，母亲节快乐！"这个乍一看，很奇怪，怎么父亲还母亲节快乐？一了解作者背景，是个孤儿，从小丧母，是父亲既做父亲又像母亲一样把他拉扯大，很感人。

诗人说，我的诗，很多人在书本里引用，比如《乡愁》《让我们从高雄出发》，我是一分钱版税没有的。据说大陆有些教科书里有我的诗，这是荣誉，我没想过要版税，但要是能跟我打个招呼就更好了，也不跟我说一声。诗的翻译很不容易，我会尽量自己翻译，像《乡愁》就是我自己译成英文的，我比较满意，一般译者译我的诗，诗的意境出不来。什么事还是自己干好。

不东 | UNIVERSAL POSTBOY

Van Gogh's art was worthless before his death, but afterward became enormously valuable because we had finally seen his astonishing imagination. During World War II, Winston Churchill lost an election after the war. He packed up and went home without protesting. He was a truly great politician. Sun Yat-sen was also a prophet who foresaw the collapse of the Qing Dynasty and the direction of the political current.

He was full of wise words and interesting ways of putting things in our conversation.

"I rarely collaborate with people in the Internet business. A few years ago, I participated in a 'text letter' contest, and can still remember some of the winning entries. 'Dad, Happy Mother's Day!' This seems puzzling, why would one wish his father a 'Happy Mother's Day'? It turned out that the author was an orphan whose mother passed away when he was little. His father brought him up as a father as well as a mother. It was touching."

"My poems have been used in many books, like *'Nostalgia for Home'*, *'Let Us Set Off from Kaohsiung'*. I never get any royalty. I have been told that some textbooks in China use my poems. This is an honor. It is not as if I wanted any royalty, but it might have been better to let me know at least. It is difficult to translate poems, so I try to do it myself. For example, I translated *'Nostalgia for Home'* into English. Other translators could not convey my poetic atmosphere. It is best to do one's own work."

Before I left, he asked how my name is written in Chinese. I said it is "Wen" as

"见"

　　临别，问我名字怎么写。我说文化的"文"，厨房的"厨"，叫文厨。诗人说，你这个名字以前没有出现过。你叫文厨，我们就在我家厨房合影留念吧。

文　厨
2015年8月6日，高雄，酷热

不东 | UNIVERSAL POSTBOY

in "culture", and "Chu" as in "kitchen." The poet said he'd never heard of a name like that before. He suggested: "Let's take a photo together in my kitchen then."

Wen Chu
August 6, 2015，Kaohsiung, Taiwan

"见"

"反省"李开复

这次拜访开复，我们的聊天就从开复患病康复后他自己总结的著名的"影响力"那句话开始。

我说，您近来在反省"影响力"，我近来却常常暗示自己未来是"地球上最著名的中国人之一"，而且人有心，天有意，是份诚实的心意。

我说，这句话我还反复推敲过，"地球上"是长城会和我必须放眼世界，着力全球；"中国人"是指移动互联网时代的中国机遇，中国人的时代抱负和世界担当；"之一"是利人利己，成就他人，塑造自性。

我说，我的这句话和你的"影响力"一词本质是一样的。我还为自己找到很多所谓积极的正能量。比如学英语，放眼世界，着力全球，需要这个语言工具，所以到今天我还能坚持背单词。我很享受跟世界上各类有独特思维的人直接

不东 | UNIVERSAL POSTBOY

"Reflecting" with Kai-fu Lee

Our conversation on my recent trip to visit Kai-fu, began with his well-known words on "influence" that he summarized after his recovery from cancer.

I said: "You have been reflecting on 'influence', while I have been telling myself that I would like to become "one of the most famous Chinese people in the world." I have been sincerely wishing for this to come true, and with God's help, it has a chance of coming true."

I also said: "I have meditated on this wish. 'In the world' comes from the necessity of the GWC and of myself to globalize, and carry out our work internationally; 'Chinese people' points to China's opportunity as well as responsibility to the world in the Mobile Internet era; 'one of' represents my wish to benefit others while benefiting myself, and to help others find themselves."

I said: "My wish is similar in essence with your sentiment on 'influence'." I have also set myself positive goals in order to help my wish come true. For example, I am learning English, because language is a necessary tool for me to become a global talent, which is what pushes me to memorize English words even now. I enjoy communicating directly with people who have unique ideas. It lifts my spirit. If I had set myself a goal to be wealthy or to get publicity, I would not have been pushed to learn English as I am doing now. In addition,

沟通，精神上愉悦。诸如发财出风头之类的目标，根本不可能激励我去背单词。由于常常思考时代抱负和我们在这个世界的担当，我对"中国人"的理解发生了变化，我们首先是地球人，然后是中国人，哪怕解决中国的小问题，也要有世界的视野、胸怀和眼光。

开复直截了当地指出，文厨你这个想法也有危险，程度不同而已。中国文化人传统思维里普遍有重名轻利的想法。今天国内很多成功的富有之人，有些还自己瞧不起自己，总觉得遗憾不能拥有名声，就是这种想法作怪。能挣钱就好好挣钱，有名誉的好事不刻意回避。

开复说："我以前关于'影响力'的追逐比你有过之而无不及。为了微博大号第一人，每天眼不离手机，开会、车上、床上，一有时间就经营。我还运用大数据，每天找出1000条最有可能被传播的微博，参与互动和转发，有时候还跟人在网上打口水仗，甚至有人要跟我约架。看着每天粉丝数呼呼地增加，真高兴，乐此不疲。我随便转一篇微博，关注度都很高，有些还抢上了头条。有时帮创业者转条微博，服务器就宕机了，你看，我的'影响力'可以帮助创业者。"

开复说："今天，我的微博粉丝是多少，我自己都不知道。我就想，这些碎片信息真有用吗？那些口水肯定没用。有

since I often think about our responsibility to the world and to our time, my understanding of what it means to be "Chinese" has changed. First and foremost, we are inhabitants of Earth. After that, we are Chinese. In order to solve even a small problem in China, we must keep the entire world in our perspective.

Kai-fu pointed out directly that this line of thinking is quite dangerous. He said that it was a difference of degrees only. Chinese intellectuals traditionally spurned material profits in favor of a good reputation. Many who have succeeded and become wealthy even look down on themselves, and regret that they are not better known. When one can make money, one ought not to reject that, while on the other hand, one shouldn't turn away from something than can bring one fame either.

Kai-fu also said: "I used to pursue 'influence' even more relentlessly than you. In order to become the biggest influencer on Weibo, I used to keep my phone at hand at all times. It didn't matter whether I was in bed, in my car, or in meetings. Whenever I had time, I would be posting on my Weibo account. I made use of big data, and found 1,000 posts that were most likely to be reposted every day, reposted them and participated in discussions. Sometimes I quarreled with others online. Some people even sought me out to quarrel with me! But I was very happy when I saw how many new followers I gained every day. Whenever I reposted something, it would gain a lot of attention, and some posts even ended up in the news. When I reposted something from an entrepreneur, their server would become paralyzed with the surge in activity. I thought, my 'influence' was being put to good use because I was helping others."

He said: "How many Weibo followers do I have now? I don't even know. I wondered, were these small scraps of information useful to anyone? Most of the quarrels were certainly useless. Some pieces of information might have been

些信息或许有用,我看其他方式也能做到,其实没那么重要。现在,想用就用,不想用就不用。"

开复说:"生病以前,每次去大学为学生演讲,难得学生热情,要求同事们尽量让更多学生参加,去一趟也不容易,每次觉得三五千学生参加的演讲才叫值得。找场地、组织演讲都是费脑筋的事情,搞得同事和自己都疲惫,其实这样的演讲已经背离了演讲的初衷。"

开复说:"你应该去找TED的创始人理查德聊聊。作为创始人,他认为今天TED的新CEO虽然把他的事业发扬光大了,成为全球会议品牌,但是今天每个TED的演讲者,都像个演员,在18分钟里,不错一个字,标准的动作,标准的表情,已经背离他们真实表达思想的初衷。"我说:"他是我在世界上"办会"的人里想拜访和请教的人之一。我也想过去请教达沃斯论坛的创始人施瓦布先生。我能感受到他们办会的"道",类似日本一些传承百年的事业之道,一种极致。"

最后,我请开复给我推荐一本书,他推荐了美国沃尔什的《与神对话》。他说这是他病中和病后康复过程中蛮有启发的一本书:人为什么存在?人为什么活着?死亡之后会发生什么?很多答案来自宗教,但宗教教义中为什么又有十八层地狱?难道我们是上天的玩偶?傀儡?这是我这个理工男唯一能

useful, but I could have promulgated them in other ways. So, in the end, my influence on Weibo wasn't that important. Now, I only use it when I feel like it."

Kai-fu said: "Before I became ill, every time I went to speak at a university, I asked that more students be allowed to participate because they were all very enthusiastic. I thought it would only be worth it if we had as many as three to five thousand participants. Because of that, it was always difficult to find a suitable venue. The search always exhausted my colleagues and myself. In effect, a talk like that had already departed from its original motivation."

Kai-fu said: "You should speak with the founder of TED, Richard Wurman. As the founder, Mr. Wurman thought that the new CEO of TED had made the conference series a global brand. However, the TED speakers of today behave like actors. During the 18 or so minutes of their speeches, their every word, every move, and every expression, is highly choreographed. This was not his original motivation to spread authentic ideas and expressions." I said: "He is one of the people in the conference hosting space that I most want to visit and learn from. I had also thought about visiting the founder of the World Economic Forum in Davos, Mr. Klaus Schwab. I want to learn the 'Tao' of their trade, like the 'Tao' that Japanese corporations pass down for hundreds of years. I want to take conference hosting to its limit."

At the end of our conversation, I asked Kai-fu to recommend a book. He recommended Conversations with God by Neale Donald Walsch. Kai-fu said that this was a book that gave him inspiration during his illness and convalescence, because he asked himself questions like: Why does mankind exist? What do we live for? What happens after we die? Many of these answers could be found in various religions, including Christianity, but why then do religions describe Hell? Are we toys of the Divine? Puppets? Conversations with God was the only book

"见"理解并觉得能合理回答上述问题的书。作者说感觉上帝给他说话，写下问题，写下答案。不属于宗教，却有宗教教义。

文　厨

2015年12月27日

不东 | UNIVERSAL POSTBOY

that he could find that gave him logical answers to his questions. The author said he felt that God spoke to him, so he wrote the questions and answers down. This book was not a part of a religion perse, but had the same essence that can be found in religious teaching.

Wen Chu
December 27, 2015

"见"

写在"文心雕龙"开号

"昭昭若日月之明,离离如星辰之行。"南朝刘勰,著书立说,《文心雕龙》,传于后世。今用书名,开设公众号,鼓励读书。

缘起和微信张小龙的一次聊天,他建议我请长城会会员荐书,每人推荐几本,数年汇总起来,也将蔚为壮观。读书之益,毋庸多说,多读好书,更为有益。近来常想,读书对于我们当前的中国移动互联网行业,乃至整个国家,亦有需要。人生有趣,倡导长城会各位会员各位大咖荐书,以期大家互为借鉴,互为启发,彼此感染,多读些书。行业从业者,若能就此形成风气,可谓乐事。

因此,我们开设了这个公众号。在思考推出这个公众号的过程中,我看到日本一则"冈森书店"的介绍,这是日本近来有点火的很特别的书店,很小很小,小到书店每天只卖一本书!店主每本书精挑细选,极尽其致!

不东 | UNIVERSAL POSTBOY

Constructing a Dragon with Words

A well-known ancient Chinese literary critic, Liu Xie, wrote about the importance of making literature as precise as possible, as if constructing a dragon in one's writing. I am borrowing the title of his book as the name of my public account, which will serve to introduce books to my readers and encourage reading.

The idea for the account started with a chat with Zhang Xiaolong, who runs WeChat. He suggested that I ask GWC members to make book recommendations. If one member recommends just a few books a year, in years, that would add up to a large number of books. I don't need to preach to you about the benefits of reading. Reading good books is even more beneficial. I have been thinking recently that reading is quite essential to the development of the Chinese Mobile Internet industry, and to the whole country of China. This is why I am asking our members, who are all very accomplished in the Mobile Internet sector, to make book recommendations, and to inspire and encourage each other to read. If this becomes a trend in the industry, then we have done something very positive.

That is why we opened this account. While brainstorming for the account, I saw a description of a Japanese bookstore, Tsutaya Bookstore. This bookstore has become very popular in Japan. It is unique in that it is tiny, so tiny that it only sells a single book on any given day. The owner makes the selection of this daily book with enormous care.

"见"

  我常去日本，日本有很多人有"道"的精神，就是我们常说的"极致"。我曾去拜访日本著名的花道家假屋崎省吾，他说自己"原本是颗女人心，却生成了男儿身"，师承家道，一心插花，毕其一生，出神入化。我去拜会东京剑道文化热心传播者松本老先生，他从日本警视厅首席教练的位置上辞职，几十年如一日向世界各地来宾无偿传播剑道，保存传统，其情可嘉。我曾和日本有着六十年工作经历的艺伎长聊，问及是什么使她做一份工作如此之久。她说，如果你喜欢一份工作，你总能找到属于你的乐趣。我喜欢倾听一些社长在宴舞时的谈话，能看到社长总是有些过人的地方，我见过本田宗一郎，等等。比如说，如果你想说自己好，最好由别人来说。

  我决定"文心雕龙"每人就推荐一本书！我想这件小事也能几十年如一日地去做，并且未来在长城会全球会员体系里进行。我会用诚意邀请我信任的荐书人荐书，也会去阅读每位荐书人的荐书，至少翻阅。荐书人及有些作者本人，或许我有一天登门拜访，也仅是这本书故事的延续。第一期，就推荐号称微信之父张小龙的荐书。因他的建议而起，也在微信首发，算是沾沾微信和小龙的"仙气"！

文　厨
2015年12月6日于北京后海木上鸟巢

不东 | UNIVERSAL POSTBOY

I visit Japan often. Many Japanese have the spirit of the "Dao", in that they push the limit in everything they do. I once paid a visit to the renowned Japanese flower arrangement artist Kariyazaki Shogo. He said that he felt like a woman inside even though he was born as a man. His art of flower arrangement takes a Daoist approach, and he has dedicated his life to mastering this art. I have also visited the Kendo enthusiast, Mr. Matsumoto, who had retired as the head coach to Japan's police bureau. He has been a tireless champion of the art of Kendo for decades. He is dedicated to keeping this tradition alive. I have also spoken to a Japanese geisha, who has worked for 60 years. I asked what made her so committed to this work over such a long period of time. She answered that if you truly love what you do, you will find joy in it. I like listening to speeches by the heads of Japanese companies. They must be outstanding in some way, having attained such a high position. I have met Soichiro Honda and many others. I learned from them that it is always better for others to brag about you on your behalf, than doing it yourself.

I decided that for this public account, each GWC member will only recommend one book. I hope we can keep this up for decades, and include all GWC members globally in the future. I will humbly invite those I respect and trust to make these recommendations, and I will read each of these books. Perhaps I will even get the chance to visit these recommenders or even the authors of these books someday. That will be a worthy continuation of the story told in the book. Our first book recommender will be Zhang Xiaolong himself, because this idea came from him, and will be carried out on WeChat. He will lend us good luck and get us off to a great start!

Wen Chu
December 6, 2015, A Café in Houhai, Beijing

"见"

《世传》一：TED创始人理查德·沃曼

2016年2月9日，世界小邮差文厨前往美国迈阿密，拜会了时年81岁的TED创始人理查德·沃曼。这是他们第一次见面，在理查德·沃曼黄金海岸（Golden Beach）的家中，他们畅快淋漓地聊了三个小时。之后，文厨进行了为期一个月，行程万里的"穿越美国"之旅，自驾车从迈阿密一直到硅谷。途中，感叹中国史学家司马迁编写《史记》的用心，开始写作第一篇千字文式的世界人物传记，简称《世传》。

理查德·索·沃曼（Richard Saul Wurman），美国费城人，1935年3月26日生于犹太商人家庭。宾夕法尼亚大学建筑学士及硕士，著名会议TED的创办人，建筑设计师，编辑出版图书约百本，生育有三子一女。

1984年，理查德·沃曼在美国加州蒙特雷小镇创办TED会议，并一直主持到2002年，后出售。TED即技术（Technology）、娱乐（Entertainment）和设计（Design）。

不东 | UNIVERSAL POSTBOY

TED Founder Richard Wurman

Foreword: February 9, 2016, "Universal Postboy" Wen Chu went to Miami to visit the 81-year-old founder of TED, Richard Wurman. This was their first meeting, which took place at Mr. Wurman's home in Golden Beach, Florida. They talked for three hours! Afterward, Wen Chu went on a month-long trip across the U.S., driving from Miami to Silicon Valley. During his trip, he realized how meaningful The Records of the Grand Historian was, and as a result, decided to write the first biography of a world-class talent--Biography of the World.

Richard Saul Wurman was born in the city of Philadelphia, on March 26, 1935, in a Jewish family of businessmen. He graduated from the University of Pennsylvania with a Bachelor's and a Master's degree. He is the founder of the renowned conference series, TED, an architect, and has also edited and published more than 100 books. He has three sons and one daughter.

In 1984, Richard Wurman founded TED in Monterey, California, and hosted the conference series until 2002, when he sold the enterprise. "TED" stands for Technology, Entertainment, and Design. It invites the wisest thinkers in

旨在汇聚科技、娱乐和设计领域的最具智慧的思想者。强调"Ideas worth spreading"，思想永恒，传播无价。

1962年，理查德·沃曼出版了自己的第一本书，阐述他们是如何将世界上50个城市构造在一个统一尺度上的。

1967年，他撰写了一本美国城市地图集。第一次让城市统计数据以可比较的形式出现在地图中。

他创作城市指南系列《访问》，通过图形和富有逻辑性的编辑方式，让游客了解纽约、东京、罗马、巴黎和伦敦等城市。

他创作的奥运会主题一书，就售出320余万册。他的《信息焦虑》一书出版后，被尊为"信息架构之父"。

他赠送文厨一本最新的著作叫《33》。他说，很多人统计我出版过83本书，但就在三个月前，我搬来迈阿密新家时，又整理出几本书，我自己都忘了。我的书大约在百本，所有的书都是源于渴望，源于好奇心，跟出版商无关，跟金钱无关，跟名声无关。

2012年，理查德·沃曼获库珀·休伊特国家设计博物馆终身成就奖。该奖项是设计界最高荣誉之一，颁授给长期为设计

these three areas to speak at the conferences, with an emphasis on "Ideas worth spreading", meaning that ideas are everlasting, and the promulgating of ideas is priceless.

In 1962, Mr. Wurman published his first book, which described 50 cities in the world and how they were built on the same dimension.

In 1967, he put together an atlas of American cities. This was the first time that the cities' statistics appeared in a map format, which enabled comparisons.

He created the travel series—*Access*, using pictures and logical editing to allow travelers to understand cities like New York, Tokyo, Rome, Paris, and London.

His Olympic-themed book alone sold over 3.2 million copies. After he published *Information Anxiety*, he became known as the "Father of Information Architecture."

He gave Wen Chu his new book "*33*" as a gift. He said: "According to some people's calculation, I have published 83 books to date. However, when I moved to this new house in Miami three months ago, I found a few more that even I myself had forgotten. Altogether, I must have published over 100 books, all of which came out of desire and curiosity. It had nothing to do with publishers, money, or reputation."

In 2012, Mr. Wurman won the lifetime achievement award from Cooper Hewitt, Smithsonian Design Museum. This is one of the highest prizes in architecture and design, awarded to those who have made great contributions to design practices.

实践做出贡献者。他个人爱好收藏,家中藏品甚丰,有毕加索素描手稿、唐三彩泥塑、印度古佛像和各国近现代名画等。

他在会谈中语重心长地对文厨说:"你也可以一辈子办会,但一定要办不一样的会!今天我不会再办TED这样的会,也不会去办达沃斯那样的会,以及所有已经有的会。再次开始,再次开始,再次开始。办会时,我什么都不在乎!没有CEO,没有总统,没有金钱,没有名声,没有权力,没有朋友,没有亲人,什么都没有!我只是遵从我自己的好奇心,自己内心的渴望!如果我的渴望就是你的渴望,那很好!但我不会迎合你的渴望,不会迎合你的地位、你的金钱、你的名声……"

临别文厨,一句赠言:没有受教,求知探索!

文 厨

2016年3月5日定第一稿于彩色沙漠

不东 | UNIVERSAL POSTBOY

He is a collector, with a vast collection including original sketches of Pablo Picasso, Chinese "sancai" statues, ancient Indian Buddhist statues, and famous modern and contemporary art pieces from around the world.

During their meeting, he spoke with seriousness to Wen Chu: "You can do nothing but host conferences all your life, but you can still make a difference in that space. Today, if I were to host more conferences, I would not organize conferences like TED, Davos, or any existing conferences. Beginning again, Beginning again, Beginning again. When I host conferences, I care about NOTHING! No CEOs, no presidents, no money, no reputation, no power, no friends, no family, nothing! I follow only my curiosity and what I truly desire deep down. If what I want is what you want as well, that's great. But I won't ingratiate myself to what you want on purpose, to your status, your money, or your reputation."

At their parting, Mr. Wurman gifted this sentence to Wen Chu: "No education, only learning!"

Wen Chu
March 5, 2016, First Draft at the Painted Desert

"见"

佩雷斯的世界和平

2016年3月9日,我和猎豹移动的傅盛、美团的王兴、优视科技的何小鹏等几位朋友一起拜访了93岁的诺贝尔和平奖获得者、以色列总统佩雷斯先生,以下内容为其本人口述。

为什么生活水平的提高反而带来更多的问题?

因为每天我们都想买新的衣服、新的车,也就意味着更多的债务。买东西都要花钱,但是大部分时候我们付不了全部的费用,所以就产生了债务,现有的工资和父母无法满足我们的生活需求以及让我们追求时尚。这种现象随处可见,例如在俄罗斯、美国,等等。

我们需要考虑的是每个人都有两种性格:一方面我们有我们的群体性,我们都属于一个群体;另一方面是我们的独立性,每一个人都想要表现自己的大众性,又想表现自己的个性,这样才不会失去自我。我们都是一样的,但每个人都是独

不东 | UNIVERSAL POSTBOY

Shimon Peres' World Peace

On March 9, 2016, Fu Sheng of Cheetah Mobile, Wang Xing of Meituan.com, He Xiaopeng of UC Browser, and a few other friends and I, visited the 93-year-old Nobel Peace Prize Laureate and former president of Israel, Mr. Shimon Peres. The following article records Mr. Peres' views expressed during his conversation with us:

Why did an increase of living standard bring about more issues?

A: Because we all want new clothes and new cars every day, we must take on more debt. Purchasing goods requires money, but most of the time, we cannot afford to pay full prices upfront, which means we borrow money. Our salaries and even financial support from our parents cannot fulfill all of our needs and desires and allow us to follow the trend, so we have to borrow money. This is a common phenomenon seen in many countries like Russia and the U.S..

We should consider the two sides to everyone's personality. On the one hand, we are all part of a group or of several groups. On the other hand, we are all independent. Everyone wants to belong to a group while exhibiting their unique character, so that they do not lose sight of the self. We are all like this. This does not mean we are all made up of two different people, but one person with two sides. We are all alike in this regard, even though everyone is unique.

一无二的。

你们都是社会主义者，我也是。我们的目标不是高品质的生活，如果只追求高品质的生活会导致每一个人的生活都一样贫穷。我们的目标是满足、幸福。你为公众服务，公众也给你一个机会表现自己。所以音乐家可以继续做音乐，画家画画，作家写作，等等，每一个人做自己想做的事。

自由表达的话题也是老话题了，比如说中国，你们想要自由地表现自己，这种自由表现所传递的信息远远超过通过谈话所传递的信息。每天我们都在说，不停地说，中国的音乐总是能反映出中国的现实，他们通过音乐表达自己的感情。但是现代社会，人们不想再表达，所以现代音乐很吵，像噪声，因为人们不想在音乐中交流了。

我们的责任是通过技术的发展使我们的生活水平越来越高，但是不能让我们的人性滑坡。

坚定和诚实意味着什么？

在我还很年轻的时候，大概24岁时，我就被委以重任，职位很高，很多人不明白原因，我也不明白。坚定对于我来说，第一就是说出真相，永远别撒谎。如果你撒谎，你会一事

不东 | UNIVERSAL POSTBOY

You are all socialists. I am, as well. Our goal in life is not high living standards. If we only pursued high living standards, we would all be impoverished. Our goal is to be happy, and to be fulfilled. When you serve the public, the public in turn gives you an opportunity to showcase yourself. As such, musicians can keep making music, artists paint, and writers write. Everyone does what they want to do.

Freedom of expression is an old topic. For example, in China, you want to express yourselves freely. This form of expression passes on far more information than conversation alone. We are always talking, endlessly. Chinese music reflects China's reality, because music can express the musicians' genuine feelings. However, in modern society, people do not want to express themselves anymore. Today's music is very loud, almost like noise. This is because people are no longer communicating through music.

Our responsibility is to raise the standard of living through the development of technology, while at the same time, ensuring that our humanity does not get lost.

What is the meaning of determination and honesty?

I was given a high post with very important responsibility when I was still quite young, around the year of 24 years old. Many people were puzzled. In fact, I was puzzled myself. Determination to me means first to speak the truth and never lie. If you lie, you will never accomplish anything, because your lies

无成，撒谎就像绊脚石，如果你不相信别人，别人也不会信任你；为了让别人信任你，首先就是别撒谎，做一个诚实的人。举个例子，在过去的几十年里，如果有人发现我撒谎了，我的职业就完了。

另一个就是要有大梦想。所有的专家都是已经发生事情的专家。不要只是学习，还要有梦想。梦想越大越好，不要害怕梦想，或者想象、创新，要大胆地想象——Don't care（不要在意其他的）。这就是坚定的两个主要方面。

另一个词语就是"批判思维"。怀疑和批判对我们展望未来很重要。曾有一个很有智慧的人说过，如果你希望别人信任你，生活中最聪明的事就是做一个诚实的人，因为诚实不花任何的成本，诚实一点都不昂贵，自大的代价却很高。在我的生活中，如果我让你进我的家门，说明我信任你。

什么是世界和平？

几年前，我们和中国最好的大学之一合建了创新中心，一个年轻漂亮的中国女生问我一个很好的问题：这个中心如何盈利？

我说，我没有办法回答你的问题，除非我们知道真正的

are like stumbling blocks. If you do not trust others, others will not trust you. If you want others to trust you, you must never lie and be an honest person. Think about what would happen if I had lied even once in the past decades--my career would have been over.

The other thing is to have a big dream. All experts are experts of things that have already taken place. So, one must not only study, one must have a dream. The bigger the dream, the better--do not fear dreams, or imagination, or innovation. Imagine courageously, don't care about anything else. These are the two components of determination.

Another keyword is critical thinking. To question and to criticize is important to our vision of the future. If you want others to trust you, as a very wise man said, then the smartest thing you can do is to be an honest person. It costs nothing to be honest, while the cost of overconfidence is very high. He said that in my life, if I allow you to enter my home, that means I trust you.

What is world peace?

I visited China a few years ago. We established a center of innovation with the best university in China. A pretty young Chinese girl asked me a great question: how can this center become profitable?

I said that I cannot answer that question unless we know what real profit is. Is it

利润是什么。利润只是钱吗?所以我想问你,和平也是利润吗?生活在和平中是否比挣钱更重要?爱是利润吗?你也许没有钱,但是很多人爱你,你会怎么选呢?完全独立,还是依赖别人?如果你告诉我什么是利润,我才能回答你的问题。是否所有的事情都和钱有关?我不这么认为。我们谈到科技和人性时,就像谈恋爱和婚姻一样,这两个是不一样的,我们是非常复杂的,爱和平静是不能同时获得的,除非你快死了。

我们应该以一种开放的心态去看待事物,我们要有自己的观点,不应该只是看,而应该灵活地看待事物,不仅仅看它的表象。我们也应从新的角度去看待这个时代,不然以后人们也许很有钱,但是很孤独。以和平为例,很多人说,你说得很对,我们需要和平,但是他们又说,你已经付出了这么多,你为什么要相信他们?因为如果你没有足够的付出,足够的信任,就不会有和平。你们也许会达成和平协议,但是那不是和平;你也许有家庭,但是没有爱,或者有爱但是没有家庭,这是两个不同但又不可分割的事物。如果一个刚起步的科技公司只想挣钱,那么我告诉你,你一定会失败。如果你没有去服务别人的想法,没有对社会的责任感,那趁早放弃吧,你不会成功的。我不是说你不应该挣钱,当然你应该,但是如果这是你唯一的目的和动机,那么你会变得越来越没有底线。所以创业者不仅应该有头脑,有创新,还要有对人的同情心。

money alone? I want to ask you in return, is peace profit as well? In life, is peace more important than money? Is love profit? Perhaps you do not have any money, but many people love you. Which kind of life would you choose? Would you like to be completely independent, or dependent on others? You must tell me what profit means to you first before I can answer your question, because I do not believe that everything has to do with money. When we talk about technology and humanity, it is just like when we talk about dating and marriage. These are two very different concepts, because we are complex creatures. It is impossible to have love and peace at the same time, unless you are on your death bed.

We should look at everything with an open mind. We should have our own opinion. We should consider everything at a deeper level, instead of looking at appearances only. We should look at this era with a new angle, otherwise people be rich in the future, but very lonely. Using peace as an example, many people say, you are right, we need peace. However, they go on to say, you've given so much for peace, why would you believe them? My answer is, if I had not given enough, if I did not have enough trust, there would not have been peace. An agreement might have been reached, but it would not have been peace in the real sense. One might have family without love, or love without family. These are two different but inseparable quantities. If a young tech company only wants to make money, then I believe it will fail. If one does not want to serve others, does not feel responsible for the world, then one might as well give up, because success will not be possible. I am not saying one should not make money, of course money is good, but if that is the only goal and motivation, then that person's bottom-line will lower little by little. An entrepreneur should have a clear mind, the ability to innovate, as well as empathy for others.

"见"

　　每一个人从自己本身来说都是很渺小的,如果你只想自己,就太无聊了。但是你可以成为一个伟大事业的一部分,一个伟大的自己。伟大的事业就是很多人去服务很多人。我们无法让事情回归原始,我们必须有机械的一面,但不是没有人性的机器。假如它是一个男人或女人,你会爱上这样的"人"吗?我觉得你不会,那是无法想象的。

文　厨

2016年3月9日

不东 | UNIVERSAL POSTBOY

We are all very small as individuals. It would be boring to consider oneself alone. However, you can become part of a greater whole, and become a greater individual in the process. A greater whole is composed of many individuals who serve others. We cannot reset everything to a more primitive state, as such, our lives are becoming automated and mechanized. But not the imagine machines without humanity, would you love someone like that? I do not believe you would. That is impossible to imagine.

Wen Chu
March 9, 2016

"见"

三 "见"

近来,我总是有些有趣的人想去见,而且越来越多,也越来越跨界、多样化,颇有点无休无止,无法收场。

我问自己,我"见"到了什么?

见天地。某种意义上,我所有会见的"大人物",都是天,某个领域的天,专家学者、大咖精英、社会贤达、奇士名流,等等。某种意义上,周游列国是见地,所见大江大河、大山大漠、名胜古迹,是见大自然的鬼斧神工、造化无穷。

然而,我沉湎于"见天地"之中,却常忘记了见众生。最近一次GMIC北京,我见众生,有了新维度。GMIC科技庙会上,在奥运训练场,我见到家长们带着孩子来逛庙会,我的心体会了过去七年来在GMIC所没有的欢乐;GMIC年度盛典上有陈伟霆、吴亦凡、范冰冰等明星艺人,现场的一条微博,转发量数百万,点击量数亿,我看见了过去七年来GMIC所没有

不东 | UNIVERSAL POSTBOY

Three Things I have Seen

Recently, I realized that there are more and more interesting people that I wanted to meet. This group had become more diverse as well, with more of them being outside the tech circle I was familiar with. In fact, I wanted to meet with so many people that my calendar was getting out of control.

So, I had to ask myself, what have I seen on my journeys, in all my meetings with all these new and interesting people?

I have seen the world. In some sense, every "big name" I met was a god in their field. They could be experts, executives, or those contributing enormous valuable to society in their own way. But traveling also allowed me to see what was on our earth, the great rivers and mountains, the cultural heritages left to us by forbearers, and the splendid world created by mother nature.

However, when I became immersed in the world, I often forgot to see people. At the most recent GMIC Beijing, I saw people, and gained a new dimension to my thinking. At the tech conference, I saw parents bringing kids to visit our displays, which gave me a joy that I had not experienced in the past seven years of hosting conferences. A Weibo post that came out of GMIC Beijing was reposted by many celebrities like Chen Weiting, Wu Yifan and Fan Bingbing. The total number of reposts reached the millions, while hundreds of millions read it. This represented a participation of the masses like never before. I also remember listening to

"见"

的众生乐。我记得在GMIC"未来峰会"上，坐在台下听科学家们讲人工智能、机器人、虚拟现实和太空探测等话题，原本听众不多的大会场安静得让人感到寂寞。我就想，我见天地有余，见众生不足。而且我现在认为，以上场景，没有高低，没有对错。

我决定从此也多见众生，天地虽大，没有尽头，众生虽小，沧海桑田！

我最后问自己，人近不惑，我有见自己吗？见自己，我却迷惑了？未来十年，我想见自己！

文　厨

2016年5月29日1000秒速成千字文

不东 | UNIVERSAL POSTBOY

scientists discussing AI, robots, VR and space exploration at the GMIC "Future Summit." The conference center was very quiet. I thought then that I had seen the world as much as I could, but I had not seen people nearly enough. I realized that both were equally important.

As a result, I decided that I would try to see more of the people of this world from now on, because even though the world was boundless, every person living in it was important in his or her own way.

Lastly, I asked myself, at nearly 40 years of age, whether I have truly seen myself. That was a difficult question to ask, but answering that question would be my goal for the next ten years of my life.

Wen Chu
Written in 1,000 seconds, May 29, 2016

三 "诗"

李白有首诗：

> 床前明月光，
> 疑是地上霜。
> 举头望明月，
> 低头思故乡。

我不知道这算不算是中国最为人知的一首唐诗，极其简单，思乡、思念亲人，最简单的文字表达了最朴素的情感。

王之涣也有一首唐诗：

> 白日依山尽，
> 黄河入海流。
> 欲穷千里目，
> 更上一层楼。

不东 | UNIVERSAL POSTBOY

Three "Poems"

The poet Li Bai wrote the following poem:

I wake up with the moon shining around my bed,
Its light glittering like frost on the floor;
I raise my head to look at it,
Then lay back down with thoughts of home.

This has to be one of the most well-known poems in China. It is simple, and expresses a sentimentality for one's hometown and family. The simplest words can often express the sincerest emotions.

Another poet, Bai Juyi, wrote the following poem:

The bright sun will set behind the hill,
The Yellow River flows toward the sea;
If you wish to keep them in sight still,
You must climb higher and higher.

"见"

这个也极简单。我都在想,王之涣先生可能就是想表达,爬多楼梯,更宜登高望远。今天被我们有所引申,人生要不断攀登,多了哲思。

还有一首诗,作者是谁,忘了。也懒得百度,但诗记得:

> 千山鸟飞绝,
> 万径人踪灭。
> 孤舟蓑笠翁,
> 独钓寒江雪。

这首诗很有画面感,有很多中国山水画,以此为素材。这首诗也很有意境,如果诗品家来个诗话,估计洋洋洒洒,能成万字文。对我来说,诗中意境,这个戴着蓑笠的老头很酷!

我就想,这三首诗,文字简单,最短五言绝句,或以情感人,或哲思启人,或意境撩人,都脍炙人口,广为传诵。

我写千字文,越写越长,越写越复杂,这样方显水平似的。最近因为工作忙,还要求自己1000秒写完千字文,化繁为简,其实也不易。有时比写长还难,难受、难过、难止。

我做长城会,工作越干越多,越来越复杂,自鸣得意,心

不东 | UNIVERSAL POSTBOY

This is a simple poem too. I wonder if the poet did not simply want to convey the benefit to be had by climbing higher and seeing as far as one can. But we are usually philosophical in our interpretation: one ought to keep going upward in life.

Another poet wrote the following poem:

Birds have left these mountains,
The mountain paths have no traces of men;
A lone old man in his straw cape and hat sits in a single boat,
fishing on a frozen and snowy river.

What a picture this poem paints. In fact, many classical Chinese artists used the poem as the basis of their paintings. The poem also creates an atmosphere that one would not be able to recreate in less than ten thousand words in an essay form. I also think the lone fisherman in the poem sounds so cool.

These three poems are short and simple, using easily understood words, but they convey such sincere emotions, thought-provoking philosophy, and imaginative atmosphere. That is the reason they have become widely known.

My own articles have become longer and more complex, as if that would better show off my writing abilities. Lately, because I have been busy with work, I would only allow myself one thousand seconds to write an article, which is quite difficult, because I have to leave out many ideas that are precious to me.

My work with the GWC has become more complex and important. This makes

"见"

力交瘁，其实是简化的功力不足，修为不够。2015年底，突然觉得自己进步了一点点，此生在商业上，成为一名俗世的亿万富翁，几无悬念，不管按人民币还是美元算。但就这件俗事而言，如果非要我不断做加法，不断把事情搞复杂，把工作搞复杂，自己的生活也搞繁杂，不是也罢，要是也得是个简单顺成的亿万富翁。

我周游列国，有时也会复杂到思考"地球上最著名的中国人之一"这样如此烦琐的问题，如果"之一"都这么麻烦，不是也罢，还是简单方好。

我人生的上半场，人近不惑，基本上是化简为繁。

我人生的中场，学习化繁为简，工作简单，生活简单，求知简单（有时候求知这样美好阳光的事都被我搞得像商业交易似的），简单做事，简单求知，简单做人。

我人生的下半场，只干一件事：清零。

文　厨

2016年6月3日早起，北京文坊千秒千字文

不东 | UNIVERSAL POSTBOY

me prideful and tired, because it is due to an inability to simplify. At the end of 2015, I suddenly found myself a little more adept, because I will almost certainly become a billionaire, whether that is calculated in yuan or dollars. But to me, if I must achieve that by making my job and life more complicated, I would rather not be a billionaire.

I have travelled around the world, sometimes meditating on complicated questions like how to become "one of the most famous Chinese people in the world." But if to become "one of" is already this complicated, then perhaps I should not aspire to this goal. I would rather pursue something simpler.

I am nearly forty years old. During the first half of my life, I have almost always made the simple more complicated:

But now, half-way through my life, I am learning how to simplify everything, from work to life, including my pursuit of knowledge - I sometimes make even this wonderful task business-like. I want to do my job simply, pursue knowledge simply, and live my life simply.

In the second half of my life, I have one goal only: reset.

Wen Chu
Morning of June 3, 2016

"见"

卡尼奇达姆

卡尼奇达姆（Kainchi Dham Ashram）是印度北方的一个朝圣场所，地处喜马拉雅山脉，毗邻尼泊尔。乔布斯的传记里曾提及他年轻时的一段往事，他去此地拜访传奇高僧尼姆·卡洛里·巴巴（Neem Karoli Baba），但他到达时，高僧已经去世半年了，颇感遗憾。他后来在这儿住了几天，获得一些启示。成名之后的乔大神推荐扎克伯格也来此地。当时小扎在创业早期遇到一些困惑，在这儿小住三天，也获得了启示。后来他见印度总理莫迪时，特别提到了这个地方，这里就开始较为人知起来。

我来印度参加一年一度的GMIC班加罗尔，每次来印度，都会选一个宗教场所走走看看，常有所感。

我曾经去过菩提伽耶，在著名的菩提树下坐了一晚，那一晚我想了很多关于自己健康的问题。当时我受腰腿苦痛，苦不堪言，身体状况急需调整。那晚之后，饿了就吃，困了就睡，

不东 | UNIVERSAL POSTBOY

Kainchi Dham Ashram

Kainchi Dham Ashram is a modern-day pilgrimage site in northern India. It is located in the Himalayans, neighboring Nepal. There is an anecdote in Steve Jobs' biography, from his younger years. Jobs went to Kainchi Dham Ashram to visit the legendary Hindu guru, Neem Karoli Baba. Unfortunately, the guru had passed away by the time Jobs arrived. It was a very regretful event, but Jobs stayed on in the area, and found great inspiration. Afterward, Jobs recommended the area to Mark Zuckerberg. At the time, Zuckerberg was looking for clarity during the early days of Facebook. He stayed three days in the area, and found inspiration just like Jobs. Still later, Zuckerberg specifically brought the place up when he met President Modi of India. After that, Kainchi Dham Ashram began to be widely known.

Every year, when I visit India for the yearly GMIC Bangalore, I choose a religious locale to visit, looking for my own inspiration.

I have visited Bodh Gaya, and sat beneath the famous Bodhi Tree for one night. That night, I thought about my health problems. At the time, my legs and my back were in pain. My body in general was in bad shape, and in dire need of a healthy lifestyle change. After that night, whenever I am hungry, I eat, and whenever I am tired, I sleep. I also try to stay optimistic, and lessen the pressure

"见"

保持乐观，自行减压，从此我没有让身体过于疲惫，一直保持身体健康。

我曾去过鹿野苑和瓦拉那西，感受到解决贫穷问题是与每个人息息相关的。印度和非洲人民的贫穷，虽然看似遥远，中国人也应担责，这是我们在世界上的义务。

这次我选择了卡尼奇达姆，从班加罗尔转机德里，德里转机到北方邦的一个小城，又辗转开车几个小时走山路，路上折腾了近两天才到那儿。因为接下去的工作安排，我只能停留三个小时，但这三个小时对我来说是难忘的。

修道所的工作人员可能觉得我这个中国人不远万里来，其情可嘉，奖赏我可以直接进入高僧的卧室禅房静坐，我就这样想起2016年来的一些人和一些事！

就在几天前的大会期间，我和同事们分享学来的财技："苦、挣、赚、来"四字真言。我说大部分人，都归为苦钱，很辛苦为了生活为了钱；有些人体力和智力好些，就会去跟人挣钱；把一块钱变两块钱就是赚钱了；最高境界就是来钱，让钱来找你。我吹嘘自己正在从赚钱向来钱的高阶上大踏步前进。在那个三小时，我静下来时，慢慢觉得有点羞愧。创业其实也是门手艺，就像那些值得尊敬的匠人，做好自己的手艺，

I put on myself. Since then, I have never overtaxed my body, and have become much healthier as a result.

I have also been to Sarnath and Varanasi, and felt deeply that India and Africa's poverty problem is everyone's problem. Even though these places are far away from China, we Chinese should take the responsibility upon ourselves, because this is our responsibility to the world.

This time, I chose Kainchi Dham Ashram. From Bangalore, I flew to Delhi, and from there, to a small town in the state of Uttar Pradesh. After that, we drove for several hours. In total, it took me nearly two days to reach my destination, but I could only stay for three hours due to work engagements after. Even so, those three hours became an unforgettable experience for me.

I think the staff were impressed that I, a Chinese person, came all this way to the temple, so they rewarded me by allowing me to go into the meditation room that once belonged to the guru. While meditating there, I remembered what I had experienced 2016.

Just a few days ago, during the conference, I shared with my colleagues the four ways in which people make money: many toil away to scrape a living together; others, more physically or mentally able, follow a leader to earn money; some manage to turn one dollar into two; while for the last rare category, money flows to them and seeks them out. I have bragged that I am on my way to the last category. However, in those three hours, when I sat down to think quietly, I slowly became ashamed. Entrepreneurship requires craft, just like those respected artisans. They take the utmost care in their craft, in making a table, a chair, a

"见"

一桌一椅，一菜一羹，一茶一果，认认真真，诚心诚意，这才是弥足珍贵的！我何时开始玩弄财技操练钱法了？

2016年初，我给自己定了一个"穿越千年"的计划，就是去世界各地拜访十位年近百旬的受人尊敬的长者。一开始，我的初心很简单，向智者见智，向长者请教。

我去请教88岁的诗人余光中，我常恐惧我所谓的想象力，所以去向很有想象力的诗人请教。诗人说丘吉尔是诺贝尔文学奖得主，是伟大的政治家，他就是一个很有想象力的人。言下之意，如果他作为政治家都可以有想象力，你一个小小创业者有什么可害怕的呢？我豁然开朗。

我去请教美国81岁的TED的创始人沃曼先生，作为一个办会几十年的前辈，他提醒我，要追随自己的好奇心、自己的渴望，没有CEO，没有总统，没有金钱，没有名声，没有权力，没有朋友，没有亲人，什么都没有！然后，他悄悄地凑到我的耳边小声说，他这几十年办会的秘密是：让参加会议的人自己多互动多交流，不仅仅是听讲者演讲。我受教良多！

我去请教以色列93岁的前总统佩雷斯先生，作为一个同时和阿拉法特、拉宾获得诺贝尔和平奖的传奇人物，在拉宾被刺杀，阿拉法特无数次遭暗杀伤痕累累地离开人世时，他何以能

meal, or even a cup of tea. They put all of their concentration and love into their work, which is rare these days. When had I started to use technology to make money for myself?

At the beginning of 2016, I made a plan for myself to "go beyond 1,000 years", which is a plan to visit ten very respected elders around the world. My motivation was simple in the beginning--I wanted to visit the wise, and ask for their guidance and wisdom.

I started with Yu Guangzhong, an 88-year-old Taiwanese poet. I have often feared my imagination, which was why I decided to visit the imaginative poet. He told me that Winston Churchill was a Nobel Literature laureate as well as a great politician. He was an imaginative person. What the poet meant was that if a politician was allowed to have an imagination, why should I, an entrepreneur, not be allowed to be imaginative? I was very inspired.

I also visited 81-year-old Richard Wurman, who founded Ted. As my senior in conference hosting, he reminded me to follow my own curiosity and desire. NO PRESIDENT, NO CEO, NO MONEY, NO FAME, NO EDUCATION, NO WIFE, NOTHING! He also whispered to me the secret to his successful conference hosting career, spanning decades, at the end of our meeting: allow conference participants to talk and exchange ideas among themselves, instead of making them listen to speeches all the time. I learned a lot from him.

I also visited the 93-year-old former president of Israel, President Peres, who won the Nobel Peace Prize along with Yitzhak Rabin and Yasser Arafat. Rabin was assassinated, while there were many attempts on Arafat before he passed away.

"见"

一生在战火纷飞的以色列致力于世界和平而享93岁的高龄？他告诉我要"Balance"，要平衡。同时要诚实，永远不要欺骗。上月听闻他去世，对这样一位老人离开，我感到难过！

原本这些探索都还好，但在进行的过程中，我开始膨胀，开始自满。我每到一个国家和地区，就跟同事说，你们当地有什么著名人物？我想见见。你们总统和总理是谁？麻烦的话前总统前总理也行，要变成以后我们长城会所到国家和地区的标配。有的说给钱就行，我大手一挥，给！钱搞得定就别浪费时间了。有时还不忘提醒同事一句，我是世界小邮差，未来几十年，这个时代，地球上最著名的中国人之一。

还有明年准备出本书，我说要请星云大师题字，请大诗人余光中写序，请大设计师原研哉设计封面，请鸟山明大师画幅漫画……这哪里还是出书，已经是出风头是作秀。原就是把过去的一些文字整理总结分享而已。现在却走向了无休无止的作秀折腾，朋友问你的书呢？两年了，我还说这是大制作，要有耐心。

离开卡尼奇达姆时，我很是羞愧。路过门前的小桥，我在桥上站了一会。看见桥下的小溪清澈见底，一群鱼儿欢快地游着。我就想，我过长江，我见黄河，大江大河，泥沙俱下，汹涌澎湃；我观沧海，我逡巡太平洋，浩瀚海洋，海天接日，无

不东 | UNIVERSAL POSTBOY

How then, had the 93-year-old president managed to live in wartime Israel, while dedicating himself to peace? He told me, the key was to "balance." It was also important to be honest, and to never cheat. I felt great sadness at the passing of this wise man last month.

These explorations were fine, but I became full of myself in the process. Wherever I went, I asked my colleague: "Who are the most famous people in your country? I want to meet them. Who are your president and premier? If I can't meet them, a former president would be fine too." I wanted meeting the head of a state to be the status quo, whichever countries I visited. Some asked for money, which I gladly gave. Time to me is more precious than money. Sometimes I also reminded my colleague that I was the "Universal Postboy." In the coming decade, in our era, I was destined to become one of the most well-known Chinese people in the world.

I am planning to publish a book next year. I was going to ask the prominent monk, Hsing Yun, to write a dedication, the poet Yu Guangzhong to write the preface, the famous graphic designer Kenya Hara to design the cover, and the manga artist Akira Toriyama to draw a few pages of manga. Rather than publishing, it felt as if I was putting on a show or a publicity stunt. It was supposed to be a simple compilation of my writing, but it became such an ordeal. My friend asked: "It's been two years, where is your book?" I answered that this was going to be a major production, so he had to be patient.

When I left Kainchi Dham Ashram, I felt a great shame. When I passed the little bridge in front of the temple, I stopped and looked at the stream underneath for a while. There were plenty of fish there. I thought, I had seen many great rivers that ran much faster; I had also seen oceans that connected to the sky. But

"见"

边无际。若天有意，我愿做偏僻的喜马拉雅山脉间这一股清澈的小溪，不羡长江，不羡黄河，不慕沧海，不慕太平洋！卡尼奇达姆，喜马拉雅山脉有一条小溪，那儿有自由自在的鱼儿欢快地游着，小溪水清澈见底……

文 厨

2016年11月23日

不东 | UNIVERSAL POSTBOY

instead of those great rivers and oceans, I would much rather live like this simple but clear stream in the Himalayans. Kainchi Dham Ashram, a clear stream in the Himalayans, where the fish may swim freely and happily.

Wen Chu
November 23, 2016

"见"

天下无霾

各位亲爱的长城会会员,新年来临之际,人在旅途,心潮起伏,作千字文一篇,诚致新年问候,祝健康快乐,阖家幸福!

接着我兼谈雾霾。

今天开车从北京出城,一路雾霾严重,令人沮丧。这次回来近一个月,在遇上一次"霾红"、两次"霾黄",因为硅谷阳光明媚空气清新,若不是如此感同身受,雾霾这件事对我来说几乎麻木了。我想起了历史上一位曾经的独裁者的一句话:我死后,哪管它洪水滔天。我就问自己:我走后,什么是"霾红"?什么是"霾黄"?

这次临时来北京,安排旧金山市市长李孟贤来京会见我们科技界的朋友和北京市领导。我很天真,以为旧金山曾经饱受雾霾的困扰,一些治理经验可以帮助北京雾霾情况的改善。然而这个月下来,我发现真不是北京一城一地的问题,真的大半

不东 | UNIVERSAL POSTBOY

No Smog in the Air

Dear GWC members,

As we welcome the new year, I am traveling. As part of my well-wishing for all of you to be happy and healthy in the coming year, I am writing this article to tell you what is on my mind right now.

I want to talk about smog.

Today, we drove out from Beijing. Smog was everywhere along our route, making us quite depressed. I have been back for nearly a month. The smog in Beijing has been so bad that once there was two yellow alerts, and once, even a red alert, the highest level of alarm. I live in Silicon Valley, where it is always sunny and the air is always fresh. Had I not experienced how bad the air was in Beijing first-hand, I would not have been very concerned with news of smog. I remember a despot once said: "After I pass away, why would I care if the world is flooded?" I asked myself, what do these phrases, code yellow and code red, mean to me once I leave China?

I came to Beijing for an impromptu visit this time around, bringing Edwin M. Lee, the mayor of San Francisco with me to visit friends from the tech sector as well as officials of the Beijing government. I was very naïve, because I thought since San Francisco was once afflicted by smog, the mayor might be able to share some experiences to help improve the air quality in Beijing. But after this month,

个中国都已经笼罩在雾霾的阴影之下。已经不是一个市长，一个科技圈，一个群体的问题。如果说，天下兴亡，匹夫有责，那么，祖国雾霾，人人有责！抱怨无济于事，牢骚更添烦恼。我们只能自救，逐雾霾还蓝天，化埋怨为行动。

我们的事业在某种意义上是幸运的，科技是蓝色的，移动互联网是立在潮头的，离雾霾是远的，总体是绿色的。我们没有包袱，我们应该大声疾呼，不再沉默，唤醒良知。当然我们不是来添乱的，我们有方法有步骤，也有能力有能量。我相信，我们长城会这群人是中国最具有智慧也最有能量的人群，至少是之一。我相信，我们可以号召数百数千的同事先行动起来，帮助各种有助于雾霾改善之工作，大家都有本职工作，但本职工作的意识里也要有治霾公益心，能帮忙就帮忙，能推动一二就推动一二。我相信，我们可以在日常工作开展中影响我们的数百万数千万甚至数亿用户的环保节能意识；我相信，我们与各级政府领导打交道时，多一份心意，积极地但也是严肃地献计献策，帮助鞭策其行动；我相信每一位的人生智慧，一定可以拿捏好这个度，因为到了这步田地，我们每个人真的是共命运，同呼吸！

2017年，我们的GMIC北京会克服万难，开辟专题，好好聊聊科技治霾，探索科学治霾。2017年，在我们长城会全球全年的日常工作中，包括印度在内（2016年11月底印度大会后

不东 | UNIVERSAL POSTBOY

I realized that the problem was not Beijing's alone--more than half of China was living in smog. A solution cannot be reached by a mayor, the tech sector, or any group. If, as we like to say in China, the responsibility for the country rests on each of us, then the responsibility to control the smog situation in China rests on every Chinese citizen. If we must trace the origins of the smog problem, we can even blame Deng Xiaoping, whom we respect and did so much for China's economy, but it is useless to complain or to assign blame. Instead, we should think about how to alleviate the problem, about how to get our blue sky back.

Our industry is lucky in some sense. Technology represents advances in science. Mobile Internet is far from smog, it is green. We are not burdened, so we should not stay silent, but should use our positions in society to call for environmental control measures. Of course, we do not want to add to the problem, so we want to be methodical and united in our approach. I believe, the GWC has put together one of the wisest as well as one of the most capable groups of people in China. We can start internally first, and start working on the smog situation by mobilizing our GWC colleagues. Everyone has a job and work to do, but we can help in our spare time to further this charitable cause that affects all of us, even if little by little. I believe we can also increase the environmental awareness of our millions of clients, and when we work with government officials, lend our ideas to help them make the right decisions to solve this problem. We have to do this, because this is the responsibility we all share, and the air we all breath.

At 2017, GMIC Beijing, will have a session dedicated to the theme of combating smog with technology, and explore what can be done in this space. We will also promote this cause in our daily work around the world 2017, including in India, where when I stopped by in New Delhi in November, the air

"见"

我途经新德里,那刺鼻的味道不亚于北京起霾时),我们都要认真地倡导治霾,并力所能及地做些工作!我在长城会同事里开始倡议"三随":随手垃圾分类,随手关灯、关水龙头,随手打包食物。我要求自己现在比以前要少抽一支烟……白云飘过,青山葳蕤,绿水长流,天下无霾……

文 厨

2016年12月30日在祖国

不东 | UNIVERSAL POSTBOY

was just as terrible as in Beijing. Let's do what we can to help!

I have put forth the idea of three little things we can easily do among my GWC colleagues: sort and recycle our trash, turn off the light and the tap, and take away leftover food. Personally, I also try to smoke less than before.

I hope we can return to a world where the clouds are white, the mountains are green, the water runs clear, and there is no smog in the air.

Wen Chu
December 30, 2016, Traveling Around China

"见"

寻梦环游记

刚刚去看了 *Coco*，我们国内叫《寻梦环游记》，是皮克斯动画出品。联想起上次在硅谷看的动画片《魔幻二弦琴》，前者来自墨西哥风俗，后者取材自日本，讲的都是阴阳两界的故事。由衷赞叹好莱坞尤其是皮克斯出品的动画，制作水准之高，令人叹为观止。

我忍不住又感慨，为什么中国就没有系统性地生产优秀动画片的能力呢？我看过皮克斯制作的所有动画片，也几乎看过日本宫崎骏制作的所有动画片，每一部值得赞赏。

真想马上就开始做"小邮差动画"，哪怕一生只制作出一部皮克斯水准的动画片。我知道皮克斯平均要六七年才制作出一部动画片，我现在做，制作出来也是人近中年啦。但现在手头的事情还有一大堆，真是心有余而力不足。

我想起，当初我邀请霍金教授在GMIC发表科学普及演讲,并与他进行了一次特别的访谈。当初实施时,这对我来说是一个挑战。但霍金教授在GMIC的演讲,引起了全国上亿人次的关注。并且我看到,现在国内有越来越多的会议开始邀请霍金教授演讲。其实这样的一种带动作用,是我乐意见到的。

我们长城会这一年来在全球发起"科学复兴"宣言,我确信,要不了多久,科学复兴一定会在全国越来越多的地方受到欢迎。

从某种意义上来说,如果国内有谁或哪个平台,能够制作出一两部真正让人赞叹的动画片,一定可以带动越来越多的人、越来越多的资金参与进来,最终百花齐放,迎来国产动画片的春天。赶紧干啊!我着急,这可是名利双收的事情,孩子们快乐,成年人也能快乐,好人爱看坏人也爱看,怎么还没一拥而上呢?

我帮这部动画佳作打个广告。这是一个有关于家庭的,一家人相亲相爱的温暖人心的故事。Coco的爸爸,由于热爱音乐,离开了家。即使阴阳两隔,他也在渴望女儿的原谅。观影时我想起了自己最近出版的第一本书——《不东》(繁体中文版),最后编排定稿时,第一篇选的是《我有一个梦想和女儿》。我在想,可能我们每个人的潜意识里,这个世界上,对我们最重要的并不一定是那些看起来最精彩、最高大上、最有名有利的，亲情、友情、爱情，以及健康、快乐这些才应是更重要的。如果我来拍部动画片，其实很想拍中国传统文化里面那些最柔软的东西，比如说传统中国的家的概念，中国母亲的故事等，以及中国传统的仁义礼智信，还有诸子百家里面的一些题材，这其实都是非常好的中国动画故事。

我又想起，马云刚刚拍了一部电影叫《功守道》，引发了一系列批评，甚至是一些扣帽子的攻击，什么玷污了艺术、烧包，等等。我倒是很简单地看这件事，马云就是一个功夫迷，自己出钱拍一部自己的电影娱乐娱乐。但立意还是差了些，功夫迷拍电影，最终表现的是把会功夫的一个一个地都打趴下，还是给自己挖了一个坑。古往今来，还是柔软的才无坚不摧，温暖的才绵绵不绝啊！

建议大家去电影院看看这部温暖人心又极柔软的动画片，我很难得为一部电影写篇千字文。

文　厨

2017年12月5日于杭州西湖国宾馆

"见"

化简为繁

中国古代有四大书院,分别是河南登封嵩阳书院、商丘应天书院、江西庐山白鹿洞书院和湖南长沙岳麓书院。这一次,我独自驾车,为期一个月,纵横中原地带,以"科学复兴"之路的名义,走访了这四大书院。

四大书院,皆历经千年,或山环,或水绕,或山环水绕。古木参天,小桥流水,鸟语花香,风景秀丽,动静相宜。程颢、程颐,史称"二程",曾在嵩阳书院讲学多年;应天书院因范仲淹读书治学之勤勉而名震天下;朱熹为官期间,苦心经营白鹿洞书院,传承至今;岳麓书院也是群贤毕至,学者云集,楚有才,斯为盛,孕育成就今日之湖南大学。

千年书院,依山傍水,或因人名,或因办学兴。学者、书生、士宦、帝王将相、奇人异士,或因书载、石刻、名山、江河,得以传世、传承、传说和传诵。他们相得益彰,源远流长。

不东 | UNIVERSAL POSTBOY

Reversing Simplification

China has four historical academies, Songyang Academy and Yingtian Academy in Henan Province, Bailudong Academy in Jiangxi Province, and Yuelu Academy in Hunan Province. On a recent trip, I drove through central China by myself, in the name of the "Scientific Renaissance", and visited these four academies on my way.

All four academies have more than one thousand years of history. They are either situated in the mountains, close to water, or both. On their premises, they have ancient trees, bridges set over lovely streams, beautiful gardens that birds frequent, and in general, very pleasant surroundings. Famous Chinese scholars Cheng Hao and Cheng Yi, held classes in Songyang Academy for years; the politician and scholar Fan Zhongyan made Yingtian Academy famous with his rigorous studies there; the philosopher Zhu Xi built up Bailudong Academy during his political tenure, and the academy has been kept in his honor ever since; Yuelu Academy had no shortage of scholars and talented people, and has given rise to today's Hunan University.

These thousand-year-old academies have become famous either due to the scholars who studied there, or due to their sought-after classes. Scholars, students, officials, and emperors, are remembered by history because their achievements have been recorded in books, or in the names of mountains and rivers. They are talked about and remembered for a long time.

"见"

我走访中国古代四大书院的行动，缘起2017年新年的第一天，我去登泰山，就在接近登顶的时候，看到孔庙，就临时决定上去转转。走进孔庙，门庭冷落，与不远处泰山之巅的熙攘人群形成鲜明对比。我想也好，图个清净，就坐下来对着孔孟塑像说，你们也挺无聊的，咱们聊聊。我说，要讲有关你们二位的大作《论语》和《孟子》，我个人喜欢《孟子》还多些，养吾浩然正气，前五百年后五百年，舍我其谁？但是现在我也很困惑迷茫，这一路来泰山，无处不霾，已经到了令人窒息的地步！我周游列国，几无过此，我是不是就该一走了之，自个儿快活去？我说，二位都是公认的有大智慧的人物，你们倒说说高见？当然，他们也没理我，我也无意再去登顶泰山，罢、罢了……

不久之后，我回硅谷，有天晚上，突然想了解现在国内大学的源头在哪儿，就找到了中国古代的书院，决定回国时去看看已经历经千年的四大书院。这有趣了，我想孔孟二位先生一定很得意，你不是想和我们聊聊吗？那就慢慢聊！每个书院都有孔庙，我就又都得去坐坐走走聊聊。还有书院里，孔孟的得意门生范仲淹、朱熹、二程、张栻、李勃、司马光、王安石、苏东坡、王阳明、魏源、曾国藩……

就这样边走边聊，我发现有个问题。这里记录的文字，基本都是繁体字。我一直对自己还能够直接阅读繁体字及部分

不东 | UNIVERSAL POSTBOY

I decided to visit these academies because on the first day of 2017, I climbed the Tai Mountain. When I was close to the top, I saw a temple dedicated to Confucius, and decided to go in. It was quite desolate inside, especially compared to the top of the mountain, where it was very crowded. I didn't mind the peace and quiet, so I sat down and "talked" to the statues of Confucius and Mencius. I said that I preferred the book Mencius over Analects, which recorded Confucius' ideas, because it alone, out of thousands of years of Chinese history, taught me how to live an upright life. However, I was a bit conflicted and confused right now. As I drove to the Tai Mountain, I encountered smog everywhere, to the point that it was difficult for me to breathe! I had not been afflicted like this anywhere else in the world. Should I leave then, and go where I can live a happy and healthy life? I said that both of you have been recognized as wise men, so would you please enlighten me? Of course, they could not really talk to me, and I was not much interested in scaling the apex of the Tai Mountain anymore, so I left.

Soon after that, I returned to my home in Silicon Valley. One night, I suddenly became curious about the origin of modern Chinese universities. I learned about the four ancient academies, and decided to visit them on my next trip to China. I believe if Mencius and Confucius knew about this, they would be quite satisfied, because hadn't I wanted to chat with them? Then go and chat! Every academy has its own Confucius Temple, and I was obliged to visit each one. There were also tributes to famous students of the two wise men: Fan Zhongyan, Zhu Xi, Cheng Hao and Cheng Yi, Wang Anshi, Sima Guang, Su Shi, Wang Yangming, Wei Yuan, Zeng Guofan, and many more.

As my tour of the academies went on, I came upon a problem. All the writing there were written in traditional Chinese characters. I had always prided myself on being able to read traditional Chinese, even some ancient classics, but I

"见"

古文原著颇为自得，但在书院也开始越来越力不从心。很多文章，很有道理，但是经过这几十年的汉字简化后，很多简体字文章，明显味道不对，有些甚至语境语意也有所改变。我爱读《史记》，我翻阅过柏杨的《白话史记》，已经堪称大师级通俗易懂的解读，但与《史记》原著之美相比，天壤之别。再想想今天台湾地区、香港地区，还是在坚持学习和使用繁体字，尤其是台湾地区，我个人观感蛮好，2016年直接受教于余光中、星云大师、证严法师、吴清友等，觉得中国文化在这群人身上很是鲜活。

新中国成立后，有多种原因，国家提出简化繁体字。比如其中有一条在今天似乎也毋庸置疑，就是扫除文盲，让十几亿中国人先识字。但是今天这一条，我以"科学复兴"的名义，用人工智能的发展，可以轻易解决。我现在正使用搜狗输入法写这篇千字文，它似乎可以提前知道我想写的下一个字或词，解决一个繁体输入显然已不是个问题。识字学会拼音就行了，我们现在每天手写的文字无非就是签名和贺卡之类。而且这些工作可以交由"当代毕昇"，像搜狗输入法的软件创作者们就可以解决。

同理，我认为几十年前提出简化汉字的各种困难，在今天科学科技大发展的情况下，大多都能克服。我们几十年的海化，就把几千年的文化积累和沉淀大规模浪费，太可惜，是该

found the writing in the academies difficult to decipher. After written Chinese was simplified decades ago, much of classical Chinese writing and philosophy no longer sounded quite right, some even changed in meaning altogether. I love reading *The Records of the Grand Historian*. I have read a modern translation of that text, by Bai Yang, who is considered a master of translating classics into modern Chinese. However, this translation could not hold a candle to the beauty of the original. Today, people in Taiwan, Hong Kong, continue to learn and use traditional Chinese characters, especially in Taiwan, I quite like that. Last year, I visited and studied with Yu Guangzhong, the monk Hsing Yun, the nun Cheng Yen, Robert Wu, who founded the chain of bookstores, Eslite, and many other esteemed scholars of Taiwan, and felt that traditional Chinese culture lives on through them.

After the founding of the People's Republic of China, mainland China adopted Simplified Chinese for many reasons. One of the reasons was to eradicate illiteracy, and help more than one billion Chinese learn to read. However, today, with the advent of artificial intelligence, I believe this problem can be solved easily. I am writing this article using the Sogou Input System, which seems to be able to anticipate my next words and thoughts. It won't be a problem to allow people to type in traditional characters. As long as one knows pinyin, one can type in traditional characters, because we rarely write by hand these days other than to sign the bill or to write holiday cards. I believe this goal can be easily accomplished by the innovators who came up with software like Sogou.

Similarly, I believe most of the difficulties of decades ago that prompted the adoption of Simplified Chinese can be easily overcome today with the advent of science and technology. This simplification meant losing thousands of years of cultural heritage, which would be such a shame. It is time to revive Traditional

"见"把繁体字恢复的时候了!

　　繁体字应该是一座桥梁。它可以连接我们引以为豪的几千年历史;它可以连接这几千年的中国博大精深的文化;它可以连接我们这个国家在历史长河中的璀璨文明;它可以连接我们中国人的几千年的智慧,有了这些智慧,在今天"商业过载"的中国,传承以及解决问题才不会是无水之源,无本之木……

　　我是长城会创始人,一个办会的。今天我看办会,一个"会"字,不是人云亦云的"会",而是这样的一个"会",她不仅仅是我个人的谋生之道,而且天地人在其中,和谐一体。是天时地利人和,是为天地立心,为生民立命……

　　化繁为简,化简为繁!

文　厨
2017年3月6日"科学复兴"之路白云山上

不东 | UNIVERSAL POSTBOY

Chinese!

Traditional Chinese ought to be a bridge that connects us with our long and distinguished history; with our rich culture; with our glittering civilization that occupied an important place in history; with the accumulated wisdom of the Chinese people over the past thousands of years, which in the overly commercialized China of today, will prove useful and practical to our continued growth and prosperities.

I am the founder of the GWC. My profession is to host conferences. Even though the simplified character for the word "conference" is made up of the characters for "people" and "talk", I believe what I do is more like the traditional character for the word "conference", which contains the characters for the "divine", "Earth", and "people." That is what a conference is, a search for harmony between all three. It is to pay respect to what is above us and below us, as well as to nourish life for those of us who live in this world.

Simplification, and now, reversing simplification!

Wen Chu
March 6, 2017, at Baiyun Mountain
On the Road of the " New Scientific Renaissance"

"见"

鸟声、钟声和名声

2016年3月,耶路撒冷。傍晚时候,我和美团创始人王兴在古城里四处转,无意中进了一个院子,院中有一棵古树,树上鸟声大噪,我惊为神迹,我们就坐在树下静听了约十几分钟。刚好有路人经过,我问原因,路人介绍这是古城一景,每天大概这个时候鸟儿回巢,都会欢叫不止,一般半小时之内结束,鸟儿休息。

2017年3月,GMIC特拉维夫和高山大学(GASA大学)一期(以色列),又来耶路撒冷。傍晚时候,我和张宏江博士相约从古城赶回酒店会合,我独自又经过那棵古树,这次没听到鸟声大噪,连一只鸟也没见到。正要离开,远处钟声响起,这次留了个心眼,看了看时间是17:33,坐着静静听着,钟声整整敲了七分钟之久。

两次偶遇,同一棵树下,相似的时间点,都是听声,这就有趣了!若简单归为神奇,不免江湖术士的伎俩。而我想借此

不东 | UNIVERSAL POSTBOY

The Sounds of Birds, Bells and Fame

2016 March, I was in Jerusalem. It was evening time, and Wang Xing, who founded the Chinese version of Groupon, and I were meandering around the ancient city. We happened upon a courtyard. There was an ancient tree there, and on that tree, many birds sang in unison. I thought it was a miraculous event. We sat beneath the tree and listened for more than ten minutes. When a local passed by, we asked him about the birds. He said that this was a well-known local phenomenon in Jerusalem. The birds return to their nests around this time every day, and sing together for close to half an hour before they settle in for the night.

2017 March, we are holding a GMIC conference in Tel Aviv, and will also have GASA University classes in Israel, so I was back in this ancient city. In the evening, I was supposed to meet up with Dr. Zhang Hongjiang back at our hotel. On my way there, I passed by the same tree again, but this time I did not hear the songs of a single bird. Just when I was about to leave, bells began to toll in the distance. I looked at my watch and saw that the time was 5:33 p.m., and sat down to listen to the bells, which went on tolling for seven minutes.

Both of these serendipitous encounters with the same tree at the same time made me stop and listen. How fascinating that is! If I call it a miracle simply, perhaps some might consider that a bit cheesy. But the point I am trying to make is that I heard the same sound both times under that tree—the sound of renown.

"见"表达的关键是,我两次在同一棵树下都听到相同的声音:名声!

第一次静听鸟声,离开时,我对王兴说,我听到了无比热烈的名声。

这一次,整个钟声响起的过程中,我努力地把自己往世俗正向去想,想财富,想智慧,想快乐……最后还是坚定地想到名声,只是加了一个修饰语,像这钟声一样"久远"的名声!

我是一个不太容易太尴尬的人,人道是自负,其实是孤独……

文 厨

2017年3月17日

不东 | UNIVERSAL POSTBOY

As we were leaving that first time, after listening to the birdsongs, I told Wang Xing that I heard the sound of fame.

This time, during the whole seven minutes while the bells tolled, I tried to concentrate my mind on worldly possessions like wealth, wisdom, and happiness. But in the end, I still heard only the sound of fame. If anything, I'd say it was the sound of a fame that had withstood the test of time.

I do not feel awkward or embarrassed easily. One might say it is because I am overly confident, but in fact, I feel lonely…

Wen Chu
March 17, 2017

"见"

世间再无霍金教授,时间永留简史传奇

最近聚精会神办会,好久没写千字文了。今天突然听到霍金教授去世的消息,虽然已有心理准备(最近我们跟他的工作团队有联系,知道他的身体状况很不好),但是知道他真的走了,还是很伤感……

2017年4月,GMIC北京大会前,我们邀请霍金教授演讲,同时为我们的"科学复兴"宣言一起发出呼吁。最终因为他的身体状况不能亲临北京,我带着团队去剑桥大学录制他的演讲,再加上他对我们收集的李开复、张首晟、傅盛、张亚勤、胡海泉及精选网友问题的答疑,我有幸对他进行了整整一个下午的近距离观察。后来我对同事说,乔布斯愿意用毕生的财富去交换一次与苏格拉底的下午茶,于我而言,见霍金教授的这份喜悦,大概就是这样吧!

为了那次与霍金教授的见面,我做了一些准备,我翻了翻《时间简史》《果壳中的宇宙》等书,基本没看懂。看了关于

他的电影，听了一些他的演讲，觉得心里还是不踏实。于是，我提前一周去到英国，专程去了他的家乡牛津，参观他读过书的牛津大学，顺道去了牛顿的故乡、莎士比亚的故乡等，只为了尽可能多地了解英国，了解他这个人。

英国的田园风光，如诗如画，人文底蕴深厚，科学家辈出，让我更加想见迷一样的霍金教授。

就这样，我以为我准备得蛮充分了，甚至颇为乐观地准备和他见面时学习他的幽默调侃几句，比如问他宇宙和女人到底哪一个更难懂些，下一部出演的电视剧是哪一部……

然而，就在我和他相见的那一瞬间，我所有的乐观、自信以及轻佻都灰飞烟灭。当这个被认为拥有世界上最智慧大脑的人，歪着脖子躺在轮椅上，咧着嘴笑着看我，那一瞬恍如隔世，不敢相信眼前发生的这一切是真实的。一个人这样在轮椅上躺了整整50多年，不是5天、5个月、5年，而是50多年啊，还能如此乐观？！他说"How are you"（你好）的时候，我完全没有反应过来，是他身边的工作人员提醒我应该去主动握个手，我才回过神来。后来，我的同事问我，怎么你和霍金教授所有的合照，以及访谈全程都没有一点笑容，这不像一贯的你啊？我现在想想，或许是我入戏太深，把自己想成了他，实在笑不出来。我想到的不是一个人怎么能如此智慧，而是一个人怎么能如此乐观和坚韧？！

我们的工作团队对他这次演讲和访谈剪辑得非常认真，中英文字幕字斟句酌，经过无数个日夜的打磨，制作完成后发给他看，他非常满意地说这是他看过最用心的一个视频。并且他专门在自己的新浪微博账号上发了一条微博，推荐大家届时一定要观看，还建议我们"科学复兴"的英文表述为"New Scientific Renaissance"，我们之前的表述是"Renaissance of Science"，显然不如他的表述精准。

写到这里，如果我就此打住，这篇千字文就算是一个很实在的名人故事吧。

我很想说说我们那次邀请霍金教授演讲和访谈的背景和目的。过去几年，因为办GMIC，我接触了科学家群体，发现科学家的思维视野和思想是非常独特的，尤其是我这个二流文科生对此半懂不懂，似是而非，但科学家看问题长远、客观而且理性。由于我当时苦恼于国内的雾霾、水污染和群体性的焦虑，等等，总觉得我们缺失了什么东西。我自己把这个归之为"科学精神"的缺失，在很多事情上我们过于短视，急于求成，结果就带来了一系列问题。于是我开始到处拉科学家帮着一起呼吁，后来就想到了霍金教授这位自带流量的超级IP（知识产权），想邀请他帮着我们一起发表"科学复兴"宣言，是有些"投机取巧"的意思。当我们联系上霍金教授，说明意图后，他的重视程度远超我们的预期。双方团队邮件来往几百封，电话会议几十次，我去剑桥大学录制视频之前，我的同事还去当面沟通过几次。后来霍金教授还帮我们发微博，将他的影像资料扩大授权至GMIC全球九站，等等。他鼓励我们要坚持做，说这件事很有意义，不仅仅是对中国，也包括整个世界……

世间再无霍金教授，时间永留简史传奇。"科学复兴"宣言我们会继续，我们很感激、很感恩有这份机缘在霍金教授的这份传奇中启航……

文　厨

2018年3月14日于北京

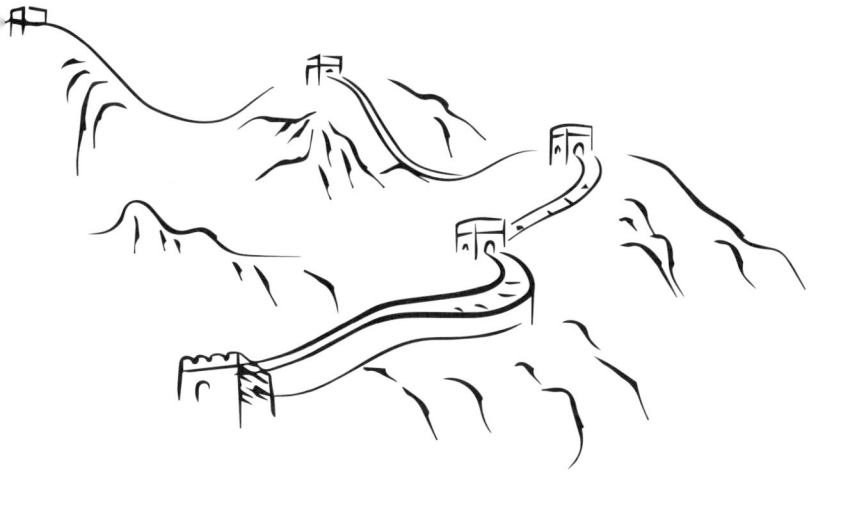

GASA大学

GMIC重大发布：筹建民间NASA

今天，GMIC北京官方正式宣布，将于4月28日在北京国家会议中心、水立方和鸟巢三地举办盛大发布会！就筹建"民间NASA"向全社会、全国和全球征求意见！

一、**名称**: GASA

GASA名称源于NASA，NASA英文原意为"National Aeronautics and Space Administration"，即美国航空航天局。

GMIC发起"民间NASA"，取意"Global Aeronautics and Space Administration"，简称"GASA"，定名为"全球航空航天中心"！

二、**使命**

为全人类建立一个基于想象力的太空探索平台！

GMIC Major Announcement: Building a NASA for the Private Sector

Today, GMIC Beijing is officially announcing that it will host a press conference at the Beijing National Convention Center, the Water Cube, and the Beijing National Stadium, on April 28. It will ask for input regarding building an equivalent of NASA for the private sector from the general public in China and around the world.

1. Name: GASA

The name "GASA" is derived from NASA, which stands for the "National Aeronautics and Space Administration."

GMIC is building "GASA", which stands for the "Global Aeronautics and Space Administration", an equivalent of NASA for the entire world.

2. Mission

Building a platform for imaginative space exploration that will benefit all of mankind.

三、发起人

长城会创始人　文厨

腾讯创始人　马化腾

小米创始人　雷军

百度创始人　李彦宏

创新工场创始人　李开复

滴滴出行创始人　程维

猎豹移动创始人　傅盛

美团创始人　王兴

Facebook创始人　扎克伯格

Snapchat创始人　斯皮尔伯格

LinkedIN创始人　霍夫曼

Flipkart创始人　萨钦

I-Mode之父　夏野刚

日本"机器人之父"　石黑浩

《人类简史》作者　赫拉利

四、三大基地

GASA将首先在地球上建立三大基地。

嘎洒镇，地处中国西双版纳景洪市西南端，素有"中国民间文化艺术之乡"之称，风景秀丽，人杰地灵。

3. Founders

Wen Chu, Founder of GWC
Pony Ma, Founder of Tencent
Lei Jun, Founder of Xiaomi
Robin Li, Founder of Baidu
Kai-fu Lee, Founder of Sinovation Ventures
Cheng Wei, Founder of Didi Chuxing
Fu Sheng, Founder of Cheetah Mobile
Wang Xing, Founder of Meituan.com
Mark Zuckerberg, Founder of Facebook
Evan Spiegel, Founder of Snapchat
Reid Hoffman, Founder of Linked IN
Sachin Bansal, Founder of Flipkart
Takeshi Natsuno, Originator of I-Mode
Hiroshi Ishiguro, Leading Expert of Japan's Robotics Industry
Yuval Noah Harari, Author of Sapiens: A Brief History of Humankind

4. Three Bases

GASA will first found three bases around the world.

The first will be in Gasa Town, a town situated on the southwestern corner of the city of Jinghong in the Xishuangbanna Dai Autonomous Prefecture in China. The town is known as the center of Chinese folk culture and art. It is also very scenic and a blessed location.

The second will be in Mountain View, California, in the U.S., next to the headquarters of Google, which many consider the "NASA" of Silicon Valley.

山景城，美国硅谷谷歌总部所在地，比邻硅谷"NASA"。

开曼群岛，长城会总部所在地，太平洋和大西洋分界线，加勒比海中心。

五、百年计划

第一个30年，GASA完成筹建三大基地，建立全球最卓越的科学家探索团队；第二个30年，GASA建立火星基地，开始探索银河系；第三个30年，GASA建立银河系基地，开始探索整个星系！

六、千年目标

地球人可以在200个以上的星球旅行、工作和生活！

七、万年愿景

地球人重建毁灭的地球，地球和地球人永生！

文 厨

2016年4月1日愚人节娱乐撰写的千字文

不东 | UNIVERSAL POSTBOY

The third will be in the Cayman Islands, where the headquarter of the GWC is located. The Islands are half-way between the Pacific and the Atlantic, at the center of the Caribbean.

5. Hundred-Year Plan

In the first three decades after its founding, GASA will complete constructions of the three bases, and assemble a team of the world's foremost scientists. In the second three decades, GASA will establish a base on Mars, and begin to explore the Milky Way. In the third three decades, GASA will establish bases in the Milky Way, and begin to explore the entire galaxy.

6. Thousand-Year Goal

Mankind can travel to, work, and live on more than 200 planets.

7. Ten-Thousand-Year Vision

Mankind will rebuild the Earth, which we are destroying, and as a species, live forever.

By the way, Happy April Fools' Day!

Wen Chu
April 1, 2016

GASA大学宣言

英文名：GASA University

中文名：GASA大学

校训：No education, only learning! 没有受教，求知探索！

序　言

当今之世界，商业"过载"。眼下之中国，尤其为过。科技时代，创新先行。科学之义，开启未来。人文思想，切实可行！

GASA取意民间NASA，启发于NASA，即"Global Aeronautics and Space Administration"，简称"GASA"，定名为"全球航空航天中心"！创立GASA University，为天地立心，为生民立命，为大学创新，为科学创造。

一

人生而平等，学而知之。知之者不如好之者，好之者不如

不东 | UNIVERSAL POSTBOY

GASA University Declaration

Name: GASA University

Motto: No education, only learning

Preface

Today's world is overly commercialized. China is especially afflicted by commercialization. At the same time, innovation is the most important to today's world of technology. Science and technology is the key to our future. Humanistic thinking has become practical.

GASA derives its name from NASA (National Aeronautics and Space Administration). It stands for "Global Aeronautics and Space Administration", meaning NASA for the private sector, for the whole world. GASA University is intended to educate and benefit all of mankind, to innovate for the entire education and university sector, and to create for science.

1.
Everyone is born equal, with the same ability to learn. Those who enjoy learning are superior to those who know how to learn, but those who take true joy in

乐之者。其要在乐学。

二

科技的根在科学，科学的翼在科技，科技融合科学，即使是商业，果实亦丰硕。

三

科技是一条道，人文是一条路，科技和人文交汇，就是一条十字路。否则就是两条平行线，永远不会相交。人类只在科技的道路上行走，就会走上不归路。人类如果只在人文的情怀里一意孤行，则永远迈不出这个星球。

四

《大学》是儒家经典"四书"之一。所谓明明德、亲民、止于至善，学习"格物、致知、诚意、正心、修身、齐家、治国、平天下"。这是古人的总结，今天的我们常常视大学为人生中步入社会打拼前难忘的一段时光，一个人的成人礼。而实际上，人生无处不大学，求知何须分年龄？

五

在未知领域，我们每个人都是小学生。世俗的大学生涯，帮助我们做一个更谦卑的学生，这是其真正的意义。

learning are best of all. The key is to take true joy in learning.

2.
Science is the root of technology. Technology is the expression of science. If science and technology can be integrated, even in business, then much can be gained.

3.
Technology and the humanities are two paths. They could either intersect at a crossroad, or run parallel to each other, never crossing paths. If mankind only travels along the path of technology, they will get nowhere. If mankind only travels along the path of humanities, they will never leave this planet.

4.
The Book of Great Learning is one of the four classic Chinese texts that illustrate the core faiths of Confucianism, including principles on how to achieve a balanced state of being, and how to learn best. These are wisdom passed down from ancient Chinese philosophers. Today, we often view our time at university as an unforgettable time in our youth before we have to start working in the real world, a rite of passage. In reality, "university" is everywhere in life, because opportunities for learning are everywhere, and for people of every age.

5.
We are all elementary school students in fields where we are not learned. The true meaning of university, then, is that this stretch of time in our life teaches us how to be a humble student.

六

这个世界上,仍有很多美好的风景、美好的愿景、美好的视野和美好的思想,值得我们探索!

七

我们这所大学的梦想:在那遥远的银河系中心,留下人类探索的足迹!

文 厨

2016年8月8日于硅谷

6.

There are many beautiful scenes in this world, as well as many beautiful visions, views, and ideas that are worthy of our exploration.

7.

The dream for our university is to travel to that distant center of the Milky Way, and leave the footprints of exploration of mankind.

Wen Chu
August 8, 2016, Silicon Valley

GASA大学颜色

我周游列国，喜欢去所在城市的大学转转。我发现大学是有颜色的！斯坦福大学是金色的，这是金钱的颜色，财富的颜色，一如这所大学造就了无数亿万富翁，改变着这个世界；波士顿的哈佛大学是黄色的，有着天生的皇家贵族范，一如这里出过无数总统、总理等政要；北大是中国"五四运动"的发源地，流淌着革命的热情，血脉贲张；东京帝国大学是灰色的，日本地震频发，资源匮乏，天生有股悲凉的深沉，忧郁的情绪；我还见过许多五颜六色的大学。

那么，GASA大学是什么颜色呢？

我认为，首先是蓝色的。就像浩瀚的星际和天空本来的颜色，是会让人联想到科技和科学，会让人觉得心无尘埃，晴空万里的那份蓝。今年GMIC首次办科技庙会，在北京鸟巢训练场里，孩子们嬉戏追逐，欢声笑语，我抬头看天，天空灰蒙蒙的，顿觉心里凄凉。我曾经专门坐高铁从北京前往南方的广州，火车行过湖南，天空逐渐蓝起来，心情也爽亮起来。我同

不东 | UNIVERSAL POSTBOY

GASA University Colors

I like visiting universities wherever I travel to around the world. I have realized that universities have different school colors. Stanford University is represented by gold, the color of money and wealth. As such, Stanford has educated many who went on to become billionaires who are changing the world. Harvard University has yellow, an imperial and aristocratic color. As such, the university has educated many who became presidents, premiers, and other important political personages. Peking University is represented by red. It was the origin of China's May Fourth Movement, full of revolutionary enthusiasm. The University of Tokyo has gray, representing the deep melancholy for Japan's frequent earthquakes and lack of resources. I have seen many other "colorful" universities besides.

So, what color should represent GASA University?

The first color that came to my mind was blue, representing the boundless universe and the color of the sky. Blue also makes one of science and technology and yearn for a pure pursuit of knowledge. This year's GMIC included the first conference of technology at the Beijing National Stadium. Kids played happily at the conference center, but above us, the sky was gray. I took the high-speed rail from Beijing to Guangzhou. When we passed through Hunan Province, the sky

样见到印度的孟买和德里灰蒙蒙的天。今天，我想这所大学首先是蓝色的，无论科技还是科学，只有蓝天的辉映，这一切才更有意义。如果商业不能辉映蓝天，我们为什么要这样的商业？

我认为，其次是绿色的。青山绿水，这是山水本来的颜色。绿色食品、有机蔬果，等等，这不是奢求，这应是天赐，这本是人力能为。这是大学应当倡导的，并应致力于解决的问题和传播的理念。群山巍峨而且青翠，小溪潺潺绿水沁人，这是不是日渐难求的果，取决于你我播种什么样的因。如果商业不能是绿色的，我们为什么要这样的商业？

我认为，最后也应该是红色的。红色代表着热烈，代表着激情，代表着火红的希望。人类生长于这个地球，遥望那未知的星际，如果我们探索星际是为了未来的人类，能够多一个容身避难之所，何其悲凉！我们因为生于斯长于斯，奋斗于斯，见证了移动互联网时代，打造更强大的科技时代，却不能向往着把人类曾实践的美好传承到更多的星球，那我们只会去糟蹋更多的星球，这样的人类就不应该拥有哪怕是前往星际探索的能力！我们人类流淌着火红的血液，有一颗火红的心，如果商业不能点燃这颗火红的心、真正人类的激情，我们为什么要这样的商业？

GASA大学，从第一天开始，我想播种这样的颜色！

文　厨

2016年8月13日于硅谷

became blue little by little, and with it, my mood became happier as well. I have also seen the same gray sky in Mumbai and Delhi. So when I think about a color for GASA, whether it focuses on science or technology, it is only meaningful if it can be done under a blue sky. If the business world of today cannot give us a blue sky, what use is it to us?

The second color that came to mind was green, the color that our landscape should be. Green food, organic fruits and vegetables should not be luxuries, but the gifts that nature gave us in the first place. GASA University should advocate and promote green living, and dedicate itself to solving environmental problems, so that our mountains will be green again, our streams will be clear. These are not goals, but future results of what decisions we make today. If the business world of today is not green, what use is it to us?

Lastly, GASA University should have red, representing passion and hope. We grow up on this planet, looking above at the unknown universe. How sad would it be if we are only exploring space so that our children will have a refuge! We were born on Earth, work on Earth, and have witnessed the rise of Mobile Internet and the making of a more technologically advanced age here on Earth. If we do not think about how to send the better aspects of our civilization to other planets, then we will only destroy those planets. We would not be worthy of the technological capabilities that enable space exploration. Mankind has red blood and a beating, passionate heart. If the business world of today cannot ignite our passion and our heart, what use is it to us?

These are the colors of GASA University that guide our journey from day one.

Wen Chu
August 13, 2016, Silicon Valley

GASA 大学

GASA大学人物

我有个聊天的方法是，会问别人最近想见什么人。一般让人随便说几个。对我来说，这的确是一个有效了解一个人近况和向他学习请教的方法。你先问别人最近想见的人，这其中可能有些他最近所思所想的线索。你从你的角度推荐他见几个人，请他也给你推荐几个人去见见，如此几个循环，你总能从这样务虚的聊天中得到一些启发。这个人的境界、阅历、视野格局越独特你越受益。问过不同人后，比较来看，你会发现其中甚至隐藏着惊人的秘密！

当然，我今天的主题不是谈如何聊天，而是分享未来GASA大学应该通过"探索"办学，会培养出什么样的人物。作为这所大学的创办人，我活用以上的方法，问了自己一个问题："中国人里谁是我欣赏的人？这个世界上谁是我欣赏的人？"很有趣，我认真思考了几天后，这些人居然与我自己以前一直以为的那些人差别很大。

先说说中国的，我想到一个人叫唐玄奘。我不是佛教徒，我

不东 | UNIVERSAL POSTBOY

GASA University People

I have a method of conversation, which is to ask someone, who have you been wanting to meet recently? For me, this has been a useful way of understanding someone and to learn from them. Asking who they want to meet is to understand what he or she has been thinking about recently. In this way, you can suggest a few people for the other person to meet with, and he or she can suggest a few people for you to meet. With a few exchanges like this, you can gather a lot of inspiration even from small talk. The more unique a person's experiences and view, the more beneficial this exchange will be for you. You might even discover some amazing secrets after chatting with different people and comparing what they tell you.

Of course, I am not discussing the art of conversation today, but how GASA University will teach through exploration, and the kind of people who will be very important to us. As a founder of the university, I asked myself a similar question: "Who in China do I admire most? How about in the world?" It proved an interesting thought experiment, because after a few days of thinking, my list ended up very different from what I had expected.

Let's talk about China first. The person that came to mind was the renowned monk Xuanzang. I am not a Buddhist, so it was strange that a monk came to

奇怪怎么脑海里突然冒出这么一个人来。或许小时候《西游记》看多了？我想到有几点他挺难得。他周游了156个国家，当然，在唐朝那样的年代，有些国家很小，他也基本在今天的亚洲版图里行走。但是请注意，那个时候没有飞机，也没有汽车、火车，他基本上靠走，靠着两条腿行走。那时候没有炸弹，没有大炮，但是山贼土匪、流氓无赖也不少，最后能安然无恙地周游156个国家，不简单！我号称周游列国，今天为止，连他零头都不到，我没仔细数过，但肯定不足56国。他把大批佛教经文带回唐朝，又心无旁骛、专心致志地组织翻译传播，丰富了中国文化。

司马迁。我认为从某种意义上来说，他奠定了今天中国人的主流史学观。我个人爱好读些历史，就是源于读《史记》。我的《千字文》中的史学观，就是学习《史记》。不以成败论英雄，项羽虽败也英雄，《货殖列传》为商人正名，酷吏伶人亦尊重其实际，等等。他虽仕途受挫，人格受辱，颇不得志，却是中华民族的脊梁。

孔丘。我个人读《孟子》比《论语》更有趣味。虽说孔孟之道，但孔子比孟子对中国的影响深远得多。孔子对于中国文化和历史的影响无须多说。但我更重其"弟子三千，七十二贤能"。为此，我创立GASA大学，希望未来"世界学友三千，和七十二个改变世界的人做朋友"！

那么这个世界谁是我欣赏的人呢？我三十岁前，没有出过

mind first. Perhaps it was because as a child, I liked the classic Chinese novel, Journey to the West? I admire quite a few things about him. First, he travelled to 156 countries. He lived in the Tang Dynasty, and the countries he visited were mostly in today's Asia. But one has to realize that there were no planes, cars, or trains then. He travelled mostly by walking on his own two legs. He didn't have bombs or canons, but had to face bandits and other bad people. Even so, he still ended up visiting 156 countries, which was by no means an easy feat. I consider myself a world traveler, but I have not visited even 56 countries. He brought an enormous quantity of Buddhist scriptures back to the Tang Dynasty, and then settled down to translate them, in the process greatly contributed to enriching Chinese culture.

Sima Qian, the author of The Records of the Grand Historian, also came to mind. I think in some ways, his work determined the basis for the mainstream view in Chinese history. I love reading about history personally, an interest that began with reading his work. The historical view in my articles came from his work as well. He discussed that success was not a determinant of who can be considered a hero, the necessity of business and many other important topics in his work. Even though Sima Qian was not a successful politician himself, he provided a backbone for the Chinese with his important work of history.

Then, of course, Confucius came to mind. I personally prefer Mencius' work better than Confucius'. But Confucius has indisputably had a far deeper impact on China than Mencius. I believe teaching was one of the most important aspects of his work. In the same spirit, I have founded GASA University, so that in the future, I can have as many students and friends who will go on to change this world.

国门。长城会这八年，周游列国后，我的观念发生了变化，开始有些模糊的世界观。所谓没有观过世界，哪来的世界观？模模糊糊地观察这个世界，就自己的发问想到了几个人。

哥伦布。欧洲有位发现新大陆的赫赫有名的哥伦布，对我来说，他最了不起的地方不是发现美洲新大陆，因为这是一个意外，其实是找错地方了。我对他最为赞赏之处是其探索海洋的精神！哥伦布一生，四次航海，对海洋的探索，无数凶险，九死一生，无限热爱，无怨无悔！有三只船，他探索海洋；有一支船队，他探索海洋；有无数船队，他探索海洋；当晚年罢官失意时，他哀求着让人带着他去探索海洋！哥伦布这位虔诚的天主教徒认为，发现新大陆是"上帝"作为他对于探索海洋的热爱馈赠的一份小礼物。

马丁·路德·金。即著名的《我有一个梦想》的演讲人，毕生致力于黑人平权的斗士。我无数次被其演说中的热情感染，《我有一个梦想》《我在山巅》等，百听不厌，激情澎湃。我常常想，到底是他的热情感染人们追求平等，还是人们追求平等的渴望感染了他的热情？或者二者原本就是相辅相成的。

写到这里，我发现以上名单里竟然无一人是商业人物。那么究竟什么样的商业人物是最接近于GASA大学的期盼呢？我想起了中国历史上那位功成身退，携手西施退隐的范蠡，但感觉

不东 | UNIVERSAL POSTBOY

Who do I admire in the world? I had never left China before the age of 30. But in the eight years since founding the GWC, I have started to travel everywhere. As a result, my view of China has changed, and I am starting to have a clearer view of the world. This would have been impossible without seeing the world first, which has in turn led to my answers to the question I asked myself.

Christopher Columbus, who discovered the New World, came to mind first. To me, however, that was not his greatest achievement, because it was an accidental discovery. I admire his spirit of exploration most of all. He was the admiral of the Spanish navy at one point, but did not mind losing that post. He sailed four times to explore the unknown seas, almost died many times, but never lost his passion for sailing and exploration. With only three ships, he set out to explore the seas. With one fleet and many other fleets, all he wanted to do was still to explore the seas. Even toward the end of his life, when he had lost his official post, he begged others to take him exploring. He was a devout Catholic, and believed that discovering the New World was a small gift from God for his passion for exploration.

Martin Luther King, who fought for racial equality his whole life and gave the famous "I have a dream" speech, also came to mind. I had been touched by the passion he demonstrated in his speeches many times, and never get tired of listening to them. I have often thought, was it that his passion influenced people's pursuit of equality, or people's ardent pursuit for equality that ignited his passion? Perhaps the two went hand in hand.

I cannot help but notice that there were not business giants on my list.

他仍然缺了点担当；我想起了德高望重的李嘉诚，知进退，懂取舍，但他缺了些探索精神；我想起了几位近几十年来的中国首富，或枭雄，或霸气，或睿智，或投机，或有容人之海量，等，但无一人能有全球视野，胸怀天下。中国人有所谓"天下兴亡，匹夫有责"，他们的天下，大都还是960万平方千米的天下！

我渴望在未来GASA大学的商业人物里，要有埃隆·马斯克的探索精神，我认为无比困难的登陆火星的探索，可以比肩哥伦布和麦哲伦曾经的海洋探索；要有扎克伯格的全球化决心，为了中国市场，谦卑地学中文、讲中文；要有比尔·盖茨的担当精神，成名美国，亦能用心救助非洲贫困、各国疾患，此为真正的胸怀天下！

大学者，大人之学也。GASA大学，探索、担当、全球化之学也。我原本以为我充其量不过是一位百年一遇的奇才，现在我想和未来GASA大学里这群独特的人共同打造千年才有的大学奇葩！No education, only learning！Have fun, be happy！

文　厨

2016年8月29日

于伊瓜苏大瀑布的源头Restaurante Porto Canoas

不东 | UNIVERSAL POSTBOY

What kind of business people would meet the expectations of GASA University? In considering Fan Li, an ancient Chinese politician who retired when his country won the war, I find him less than responsible. In considering Li Ka-shing, who knew when to step back and give up something, I find him lacking in the spirit of exploration. In considering the wealthiest Chinese people of the last few decades, who were all different, I find that none of them had a worldly mentality. A Chinese proverb said that the welfare of the world is everyone's responsibility. But for most of these wealthy Chinese, their world was still just China.

I hope that the business people that GASA University esteems in the future, will have a spirit of exploration like Elon Musk. Today's exploration of Mars is comparable to the explorations of Columbus and Magellan. These business people should also be global like Mark Zuckerberg, who learned Chinese for his venture into China. They should also have social responsibility at the forefront of their minds like Bill Gates, who succeeded in the U.S., but has dedicated his subsequent work to alleviate poverty in Africa and curing diseases around the world. The world includes all corners of this planet.

The word "university" means "great learning" in Chinese. GASA University should be a global exploration and learning. I used to think that I am a uniquely talented person, but with GASA University and the team I have gathered, we can help to make many more uniquely talented people in the future. No education, only learning! Have fun, be happy!

Wen Chu

August 29, 2016,Restaurante Porto Canoas, at the Source of the Iguazu Falls

GASA大学方针

GASA大学的十二字方针是：科学探索、公益心态、商业方法。

何谓科学探索？科学即分科而学。可定性，可定量，可论证，可推敲。中国古语"格物"即科学，以格物致知。即使科学，常常也无法致知，那么无穷无尽的科学探索，其本身便具有了意义。

当今世界，商业过载；今之中国，尤其为过！我周游列国，求知探索，远思中华五千年文明，近观美利坚峥嵘数百年，困惑不解，混沌无知。硅谷安静，夜观天象，数星望月，隐约之间，指向科学！

人近四十，总想"不惑"一切。去教堂礼拜，去寺庙烧香，我也都做过，终不及科学之实际，不及格物之致知。宗教、人文、艺术、政治和商业等，唯有科学更纯粹。或者说，

不东 | UNIVERSAL POSTBOY

GASA University Guidelines

Our guidelines are scientific exploration, mentality for public welfare, and Commercial methods.

What is scientific exploration? Science is a definitive subject, one that can be proved and can withstand scrutiny. It is a study of the physical world, a study to further learning, so scientific exploration is meaningful in itself.

We live in an overly commercialized world, especially China. I have travelled around the world in pursuit of learning and exploration. I have thought about China's five thousand years of history, as well as the U.S.' brief but illustrious one, in order to gain insight. It is quiet in Silicon Valley, where I can watch the night sky, look at the moon and the stars, and find myself infinitely closer to science.

I am nearly 40-years-old, an age that the Chinese traditionally considered will finally understand the world. I have gone to worship in churches and temples, but neither is as practical as science or as meaningful to learning. Science is purer than religions, humanities, art, politics, and business. Or rather, it would be more

以科学更纯粹地观照以上种种，更相得益彰。

我是一个文学青年，今天却要以科学的名义创立GASA大学，我自己都觉得奇怪。但似乎这个世界上那些最好的大学，也不都是教育家创立的。而且，我想从GASA大学创立的第一天，就找到这个地球上最好的科学家来做老师，以他们为主体，而不是商业世界的领袖。做个比喻，如果GASA大学未来是地球上所有大学中的"皇冠"，那么这个皇冠中最为耀眼的"明珠"就是那些科学家。这对我个人实际背景来说，也很有趣！今天，我们招募最具有商业潜能的创业者来学习，却邀请几乎是最缺乏商业思维的科学家们来授课，这会是什么样的商业远景，什么样的科学探索？

为什么是公益心态？教育即公益。人类这几千年的文明，教育之公心为最！医生救人生死病痛，为人师长者关乎人心关乎灵魂，比之救助人之躯体者，更为深远！

今年初，我给自己定了一个"穿越千年"的计划，就是去这个世界拜访10位年近百岁的长者，求知解惑。我去拜访88岁的大诗人余光中老师，在他家中的3个小时，他为我的"想象力"解了惑。从小到大，我就爱胡思乱想，这几年，创业维艰，商业上讲究严谨、逻辑严密，常常担心自己所谓的想象力，折腾自己也折腾他人，让自己和大家的心血付诸东流。诗

beneficial if we can consider the above subjects with a more scientific and purer approach.

I have always been interested in arts and humanities, but I am founding GASA University based on science. That sounds a bit strange even to myself. But it seems that the best universities of the world were not founded by educators. I want to assemble a team of the best scientists in the world to be our professors, instead of a team of business leaders. If GASA University will be a crown of our world in the future, then the scientists will be the brightest gems on that crown. This is pretty interesting, considering my own background. We are recruiting the innovators with the most business potential to study at GASA, but we are inviting scientists, who do not think with a business approach. What kind of scientific exploration will result from this experiment?

What is a mentality for public welfare? Education is public welfare, and it has been the most important accomplishment in mankind's history. Doctors cure our bodies, but teachers take care of our souls, which has a broader impact.

At the beginning of the year, I made the plan to time travel through the millennium, which is to say, I visited ten elders close to 100-years of age around the world, to see what I can learn from them. I visited the 88-year-old Taiwanese poet Yu Guangzhong, and spent three hours with him. He answered my question on imagination. I had always had an overly active imagination. In recent years, I have been an entrepreneur. One should be careful in the business world, so I have worried that my imagination would prove harmful to business and our work. The poet did not answer my question straightaway, but gave me an example. He asked me to consider the highly imaginative politician, Winston Churchill, who solved political problems with imagination. What the poet meant was that if

人根本就没有正面回答我的这个问题，只是举了一个例子。他说，有一位伟大的颇具想象力的政治家丘吉尔，解决政治问题也擅长运用想象力，不仅仅是在他的文学作品中。言下之意，政治都可以，何况商业？我去美国迈阿密拜访81岁的TED创始人理查德·沃曼先生，在他家中的3个小时，他为我对于渴望与热情的理解解了惑。我对于"地球上最著名的中国人之一"的渴望是错的，但不要压抑渴望；热情过了头，但不要挫伤热情。探索不止，求知不息。No education, only learning！没有受教，求知探索！我借用了这句话作为GASA大学的校训。

我想如果更多人都可以有这样的3小时，那么很多更有悟性的人可以更为受益！今天，我们诚意邀请美国顶尖的科学家们每个人能挤出他们宝贵的3小时，为GASA大学的同学们授业解惑。同时，邀请这个世界上我们心目中最卓越的那些智者，可以每年留给这所全球流动的大学3小时！

唯有公益心态，我们才有机会赢得这份心意！我问自己，从今往后，我是否有这样的公心，愿分享自己人生中这样的每一个3小时机会，化成知识的桥梁，连接GASA大学里每一位同学，而我就是其中的一位学生。

商业方法。既然商业过载，为何又提商业方法？过犹不及，不是商业之过，商业本身是最优的效率、最佳的配置和最

imagination is useful even in politics, why can it not be useful to me in business? I also visited Richard Wurman, the 81-year-old founder of TED, in Miami. He answered my questions regarding desire and passion in the three hours I spent with him. He said that it was wrong of me to want to become the most famous Chinese person in the world, but it also would not do to suppress this desire. I was too passionate, but it was not right to stifle this passion. Exploration and learning never end. No education, only learning! I am borrowing this sentence for the motto of GASA University.

If others could have three hours with these wise elders like I did, they could have benefitted greatly as well. With this in mind, we are inviting the top scientists in the U.S., and asking them to give us three hours out of their precious time, to teach GASA students and answer their questions in the same way. We are also inviting the wisest people in the world to give GASA University three hours every year for the same purpose.

This is only possible with a mentality for public welfare. I hope that I will share all of these three-hour opportunities for learning in my life, and act as a bridge that connects each of our students, myself included, with knowledge and learning.

Why do I bring up commercial methods if I think the world is already overly commercialized? Commercializing itself means the highest efficiency, the most optimal combination, the best organization abilities and many other "optimal" methods. It is the obeying of market patterns to find the best methods, so it goes hand in hand with humanity and regulations. As such, we should learn how to

好的组织能力等。商业是遵循市场规律来有效配置资源，好的商业方法，本质上是符合人性、尊重市场规律的制度安排。为此，商业方法我们需要学习，需要研究。举个例子，我提出GASA大学，我们要在商业运营上也是成功的，我们给科学家们招募到全球最具潜质的创业者，向科学探索致敬；我们要在世界各地最美好的校舍学习；我们要有世界各地最有效最有保障的教学条件，因为我们最为宝贵的时间，都要全心全意聚精会神用来求知，用来探索！

No education, only learning！

文　厨

2016年9月10日于硅谷

顺致全球的老师们节日快乐

operate in the same optimal fashion. Take GASA University as an example. We are commercially successful. We gather the innovators with the highest potential to learn from the best scientists and pay respect to scientific exploration. We will be learning on the most beautiful campuses around the world. We will have the most efficient teaching methods, because we want to use all of our most precious time to learn whole-heartedly, and focus all of our attention on exploration.

No education, only learning!

Wen Chu
September 10, 2016, Silicon Valley
Wishing Teachers Around the World, Happy International Teachers' Day!

GASA大学使命

中秋,月圆之夜,硅谷赏月,诗情画意!什么是GASA大学之使命?举头望明月,闲庭信步。侧耳听水流,才思泉涌。

Explore the universe and make a better earth!

近来常想,"Change the world"(改变世界)几乎是每个地球人的口头禅。但我们为什么一定要改变些什么才罢休呢?科技进步,经济发展,但似乎世界和平没有进步也没有发展。脸书、微信和谷歌横空出世,信息过载,知识爆炸,但地球人的文明真的是一日千里?

No education, only learning! 没有受教,求知探索!No changing, only exploring! 只求探索,莫问改变!探索之中自有改变,探索宇宙,让地球更美好!1492年,哥伦布探索海洋,发现新大陆;500年后,探索星际,人类的发现才更具有无穷无尽的想象!

不东 | UNIVERSAL POSTBOY

GASA University Mission

It is Mid-Autumn Festival, a time when the moon is perfectly full. I am appreciating the moon from Silicon Valley and feeling very poetic. What is the mission of GASA University? That is the question I am considering as I look at the moon from my beautiful garden.

Explore the universe and make a better earth!

I have been thinking recently that "change the world" is on everyone's tongue, but why must we change something? Technology has made great advances, and economics has developed, but we seem to have made little progress for world peace. Facebook, WeChat, and Google have been born, causing an explosion of information and knowledge, but has that led to a true advance in our civilization?

No education, only learning! No changing, only exploring! Exploration contains change. Exploring the universe will inevitably make Earth a better place. In 1492, Christopher Columbus explored the seas and discovered the New World. Five hundred years later, we are exploring the universe, and our discoveries have surpassed our wildest imagination.

GASA 大学

　　未来数十年，GASA大学汇聚地球上最具远见的科学家，科学是人类探索星际最切实可行的钥匙；汇聚功成名就的企业家与投资家，以商业智慧有效地配置社会资源探索星际；汇聚任期届满的政治家，凝聚人心，探索星际！

　　未来数百年，GASA大学建立人类在地球之外的若干探索基地，不分国家和地区，不分民族，不分宗教信仰，不论NASA，不论酒泉，不论俄罗斯联邦航天局，共享平台，共享星际探索的知识和资源，以整个人类的福祉共享一切！

　　未来数千数万年，GASA大学以地球万物生灵之名，担当，奋斗，涅槃，一起完成人类自我救赎！

GASA大学，如果有一个人，我们探索星际；
GASA大学，如果有一组人，我们探索星际；
GASA大学，如果有一群人，我们探索星际！

Explore the universe and make a better earth！

文　厨
2016年9月15日中秋夜于硅谷

不东 | UNIVERSAL POSTBOY

In the coming decades, GASA University will gather the most visionary scientists in the world. Science is the most practical key to space exploration. We will also gather the most accomplished entrepreneurs and investors, to put together the most efficient combination of resources to explore the universe. We will gather former politicians of the world, so that everyone on Earth will be inspired to explore the universe as a united force.

In the coming centuries, GASA University will establish bases of exploration outside Earth. These bases will not be segregated by countries, races, religions. Everyone will share these bases and share the knowledge and resources for space exploration. It will benefit the entire humanity.

In the coming millennia, GASA University will be responsible for all living beings on Earth, and strive for the self-redemption of mankind.

If GASA University has one person, we will explore the universe.
If GASA University has a group of people, we will explore the universe.
If GASA University has many more people, we will explore the universe!

Explore the universe and make a better Earth!

Wen Chu
September 15, 2016, Silicon Valley Mid-Autumn Festival,

GASA大学：人类的最高学府

GASA即Global Aeronautics and Space Administration，全球航空航天中心。GASA大学即全球航空航天中心大学，致力于打造人类的最高学府，让人类成为多星际物种！

GASA源于一个2016年4月1日愚人节的千字文故事，聚集全人类的智慧、知识和资源来研究和探索星际，所有成果全开放全透明，只有一些"愚人"过节时才相信的故事。

GASA大学于2016年8月8日在硅谷发起，"GASA大学宣言"中提出"No education, only learning"，没有受教，求知探索！第一批授课科学家教授有张首晟、杨培东、鲍哲南、李飞飞、汤姆·米切尔等；分享讲师有：理查德·沃曼、克里斯·安德森、隈研吾、余承东、李开复、傅盛和周航等；首期学员有文厨、赖奕龙、傅盛、葛琦、李琦、郝义和王强宇等23名。一切"无中生有"，从零到一。

不东 | UNIVERSAL POSTBOY

GASA University: Institution for the Highest Learning for Mankind

"GASA" stands for Global Aeronautics and Space Administration. GASA University means the university dedicated to Global Aeronautics and Space Administration, an institution for the highest learning for mankind, and allowing mankind to become a multi-planetary species in the future.

This name originated on April 1, 2016. I wrote an article that day that promised to gather the wisdom, knowledge, and resources of all of mankind, to make all achievements entirely open and transparent, an aspiration that perhaps seems unbelievably grand.

GASA University originated on August 8, 2016, in Silicon Valley. The motto "No education, only learning" originated in an article I wrote entitled "GASA University Declaration." Our first group of scientist-professors include Zhang Shousheng, Yang Peidong, Bao Zhenan, Li Feifei, Tom Mitchell, and many others. Our lecturers include Richard Wurman, Chris Anderson, Kengo Kuma, Yu Chengdong, Kai-fu Lee, Fu Sheng, Zhou Hang, Our first group of 23 students include myself, Wen Chu Lai Yilong, Fu Sheng, Ge Qi, Li Qi, Hao Yi, and Wang Qiangyu. It was a fresh start.

GASA 大学

值此辞旧迎新之际,作千字文一篇,世界小邮差立志投身GASA大学教育探索事业,为天地立心,为生民立命,为往圣继绝学,为万世开太平!祝大家圣诞快乐,健康平安!

文 厨

2016年12月24日平安夜于北京

不东 | UNIVERSAL POSTBOY

At this time of great change, I wrote this article as the "Universal Postboy" who will dedicate his life to the exploration of GASA University, with a worldly view, an intention to benefit all of mankind, and a conviction to explore the greatest unknown. Wishing everyone perfect health and Merry Christmas!

Wen Chu, Beijing
December 24, 2016, Christmas Eve

致GASA大学2017级同学

各位同学,大多数已为人父的你,节日快乐!

今天小酌了几杯,借机跟大家聊聊我们的GASA大学。我们这30位同学会是教育史上的传奇,我作为第一位GASA大学报名入学的学生,想说说为什么我们会成为传奇。

首先我们这所"三无大学",没有校长,我不是校长,40岁的我创办这所大学,虽然事实上承担了部分"校长"的职责,但我深知还差得远呢!未来40年,我立志成为这个时代最伟大的校长之一。

No education, only learning! 就像我们的校训,一切事物的本质就是求知,就是探索!我在探索这个时代什么样的人物才堪称最伟大的校长!

我们没有教授,但我们邀请这个世界上最好的教授、最好

不东 | UNIVERSAL POSTBOY

To the Class of 2017 of GASA University I

Since many of you are fathers like myself, let me start by wishing you: Happy Father's Day!

I had a few drinks today, and wanted to take this opportunity to talk to you candidly about GASA University. I believe our class of 30 students will become something of a legend in the history of education. As the first student to enroll in GASA University, allow me tell you why.

First, Compared to traditional universities, there are three things GASA University does not have. we do not have a president. I am not the president of the university. I founded the university at the age of 40, and even though I do undertake parts of the responsibilities that a president would, I know that I am far from being ready to be the president. However, in the next four decades, I am determined to become one of the greatest university presidents of our age.

Our university motto is "No education, only learning!" Indeed, the essence of learning is a tireless quest for knowledge, and constant exploration of the world. What I will be exploring is this: what kind of person is worthy of being considered the greatest university president of our age?

的科学家,来为我们授课。我尝试以最大的热忱邀请有识之士成为我们的校董:张宏江、李开复、鲁白、汤姆·米切尔、王坚、张首晟、杨培东和沈南鹏,他们就是我心目中最好的教授和校董!以前开复是我的偶像,今天我看他却是可爱,突然来个冷幽默,哪里像个偶像啊!宏江以前在我心目中就是一个成功的职业经理人,但是他参与GASA大学的工作这段时间,他的那股认真劲让我肃然起敬,认真的人真有趣!缠不过我的沈南鹏,一句文厨兄,我同意做校董,跟着你一起探索科学啦!有时候真是感叹,人生中有这么一群有趣可爱的人一起探索无尽的未知,这份喜悦就弥足珍贵!

没有校舍,我们选择现在这个世界上最美的校园、最妙的场景来作为求学之所,这本身也很有意思。

然而,还是要给GASA大学2017级同学们最热情最热烈的掌声,我们从创立的第一天,就提出"一切以学生为中心"!我在求知探索的过程中,请教那些最伟大的校长们,约翰·亨尼斯、理查德·莱文和俞敏洪等,无一例外地提到学生是一所学校最为重要的。印奇说,我欣赏文厨,我加入。这就是我心目中最好的学生,最好的同学,年轻、聪明、有梦想!梁信军,这位出众的企业家同学我们见面不多,我个人颇为惊讶,他为什么选择未来几年参与GASA大学的求学和探索?程维告诉我,"五一"假期期间,他基本没出门,主要就是学习

Second, we do not have professors either. But we are inviting the world's foremost scholars and scientists to teach us. I have personally invited some of the most accomplished people of our age to be the trustees of our school: Zhang Hongjiang, Kai-fu Lee, Lu Bai, Tom Mitchell, Wang Jian, Zhang Shousheng, Yang Peidong and Shen Nanpeng. To me, they are the best trustees for our university. Kai-fu Lee was my idol, but now I know that more than that, he is a funny and approachable man--a friend. I knew Zhang Hongjiang was successful in management, but since he has taken part in GASA University, I saw how he took all of his responsibilities very seriously, which commanded my respect. How fascinating people are, when they are working seriously! Shen Nanpeng, who could not resist my repeated invitations, finally said, simply: "Yes, Wen Chu, I will be a trustee of the university and explore the science field with you." I have thought often that just being able to explore our boundless unknown universe alongside such an interesting and lovely group of people is a joy worth cherishing on its own.

Last, we do not have a campus. Instead, we select the most beautiful campuses in the world as our places of learning, which has proven to be a very interesting choice as well.

Having said all of that, allow me to offer my warmest and most enthusiastic round of applause to you, the students of the Class of 2017. Since the inception of the university, we have decided that everything at GASA University would be "student centered." This was what all the distinguished university presidents I have asked for advice from, including John Hennessy, Rick Levin and Yu Minhong, told me as well. One of our students, Yin Qi told me: "I respect your work and your mission, Wen Chu. So I am in." To me, he represents the ideal GASA University student and the type of person I want to study with: an intelligent young person with enormous passion. I only met with Liang Xinjun,

GASA大学的往期课程。李琦同学，过去几期短期班，每次必到，每次综合排名都第一，在GASA大学为其求学生涯未有之投入……

GASA大学2017级同学，我们想怎么干？最近与张宏江等校董商量，我也常常日思夜想，更新了最新思路：

科学优先。GASA大学起因就是我发现科学居然也这么美妙，亲爱的科学家原来也可以是亲切而有爱的。我是一个二流文科生，这样的反差鲜明而强烈，过去几期短期的尝试，同学们皆以为可，为此我也一发不可收拾，还呐喊"科学复兴！"霍金教授再来一句洋文"New Scientific Renaissance"（科学复兴），我这位完全不懂科学的学生也就成为科学的发烧友。

全球优先。我曾自以为是地总结，"你中有我，我中有你"才是真正的全球化。年轻的我认为，中国优先的前提必须是世界优先，虽然我还是认为祖国万岁，但是前提还得是地球万岁！所以我们选择八个国家和地区进行求学探索，中国，我亲爱的祖国，是其中一站。硅谷的创新、印度的文明、以色列的宗教、日本的长久之道、英国的近现代文化、巴西的亚马孙等都需要真诚以待！

很期待，和各位成为同学以这样一种前所未有的方式，以

another student who is an outstanding entrepreneur, a few times, so I was quite surprised that he decided to participate in GASA University for the next few years. Our classmate, Cheng Wei, told me that during the May 1st week-long Chinese national holiday, he hardly left his house. Instead, he decided to catch up on past GASA University courses. Li Qi, who never missed a single class and had the best score every time, said he had never had to work as hard as he did for GASA University classes.

So, Class of 2017, what do we want to do? I have been discussing this with Zhang Hongjiang and some of our other trustees, as well as meditating on this topic on my own. My latest thinking is as follows:

Prioritize science. I founded GASA University when I realized that science can be extremely elegant, and scientists are personable and friendly people. I have always considered myself a second-rate liberal arts student, very different from scientists. But after a few semesters of trial classes, I have fallen in love with science. As Prof. Stephen Hawking said, we are in a "New Scientific Renaissance." I have become a huge enthusiast for science and a champion for scientific research.

Prioritize globalization. I always thought true globalization is possible only when the entire world is integrated as one. I believe that to prioritize China, we have to prioritize the world first. In other words, even though I love my country, our planet as a whole has to come first. As such, we selected eight countries in which to carry out our learning and exploration. This list includes China, of course, but we also place enormous value in the U.S. for its innovation, India for its rich culture, Israel as the birthplace of three major religions, Japan for the long-term visions of its corporations, the U.K. for its modern and contemporary development, Brazil for the unique environment in the Amazonian Jungles, as well as Taiwan for its traditional Chinese cultural heritage.

这样一种无与伦比的尝试,以这样一种畅快淋漓的探索……No education, only learning!

文　厨

很自豪的GASA大学创办人2017年6月17日于硅谷

不东 | UNIVERSAL POSTBOY

I am very much looking forward to this experiment that has never been conducted before, an experiment that will be carried out alongside all of you, an experiment that is all about our quest for knowledge, and our exploration of the unknown.

No education, only learning!

Wen Chu, the Proud Founder of GASA University, Silicon Valley
June 17, 2017

GASA 大学

再致GASA大学2017级同学

今天和大家聊聊我们GASA大学2017级求学探索的具体思路。

"一切以学生为中心",这是我们的指导原则。基于这个原则,我们从这几个方面展开工作:

一、招募最好的学生

这也是我们为什么把一期学生的数量上限定为30名。若不是考虑必要的成本因素,我个人甚至更为偏执地认为,十几二十人会更接近求学的本质。都说一个7个人的工作团队是最有效率的团队,我认为同学彼此之间容易记住每一位同学的名字很重要,这样的求学集体才有可能成为一个取长补短、团结友爱的亲密集体。目前我们没有对外公开招生,基本上是我个人一一邀请,最近我们会酌情开放给校董们推荐学生。某种意义上,我们是"关门"的,宁缺毋滥。我一直在思考,今天连接

不东 | UNIVERSAL POSTBOY

To the Class of 2017 of GASA University II

Today, I want to talk more about the specific ideas we have for the Class of 2017, in terms of the curriculum and focus of the program.

Our guiding principle is that everything should "student centered." With this in mind, we are designing the program in the following ways:

First, we want to recruit only the best students.

This is the reason that each of our classes will have at most, 30 students. In fact, if cost-efficiency was not a concern, I would have preferred to have only less than 20 students, which I believe is the ideal class size for learning. It has been said that a team of seven is the most efficient. Along these lines, I believe that it is very important for our students to be able to learn each other's names without difficulty. In this way, our student body will be an intimate group where everyone is integrated, and our strengths and weaknesses complement each other. As of now, GASA University is not open to the general public. Instead, I have personally extended an invitation to each of our students. In the near future, we will also give our trustees leave to recommend students personally. As such, we are extremely selective with our recruitment process. I have always thought that

十几亿人的Facebook，如果没有从哈佛的"封闭校园"开始，或许就没有今天的Facebook。我在想，未来十年，或许我们都需要是"闭门"的。十年或许听起来有点夸张，但参照牛津大学的千年历史来看，作为一所大学开创前期的谨慎态度，这不为过。一颗种子决定未来的参天大树，所谓环境、所谓人力和所谓资源等都在其次。我们视未来十年我们这群人，某种意义上就是"GASA大学的种子"，所以不得不慎之又慎啊！十年树木，百年树人，千年树学校！为了未来长长久久彻彻底底地"开门"，今天我们必须坚持坚决地"关门"，认真准备，悉心呵护，招募最好的学生，不在多，一个都行，一期最多三十人！

二、邀请最好的教授

有了"一切以学生为中心"这一指导原则，邀请最好的学生，这时候再来看什么是"最好的教授"。其实也简单，就是学生们最喜欢的教授优先，一开始可以以"名声"为雷达。一般来说，名声越大学问越大，如果"名不符实"，不是约定俗成的"实名"教授，我们很快可以辨识出来，做出筛选即可。有真才实学但不出名的教授，我们以自己的方式给以最高的礼遇！

不东 | UNIVERSAL POSTBOY

FaceBook could not have grown to this massive network of more than 100 million people if it had not started in the relatively closed-off and selective environment of Harvard University. So in the coming decade, we need to close off the GASA University network in this sense as well. Ten years might seem like a long time, but if one considers Oxford University's more than one thousand years of history, it is not difficult to see that it is best to be a little cautious in the beginning stages of a university's formation. The quality of the seed is the most important factor that determines how tall a tree can grow. Similarly, the earliest form of a school is far more important to its success than other factors like the environment, its human capital, and its other resources. To GASA University, our current class is its seed. So of course we have to extremely careful. We want the school to be truly open and inclusive in the future, but to achieve this goal, we have to be more selective for now. We will use this space of time to make careful preparations, and nurture the school and our students with infinite care. With this in mind, one student is sufficient, 30 is more than enough and as many as we will have right now.

Second, we want to invite only the best professors.

With our "student centered" approach in mind, we have only accepted the best students. So then, who would be the most qualified professors to teach our excellent students? This is simple as well, in fact. We will invite the professors from whom our students are most eager and excited to learn. In the beginning, we can use a professor's academic reputation as a guidepost--the more renowned a professor is, the more qualified he is. In cases of those who do not deserve their renown, those who are not in actuality the most qualified professors, I believe we would be able to easily recognize them and remove them from our faculty. But we will also be sure to treat those talented professors who may not be as well-known with the highest levels of respect as well.

Third, we believe that enlightenment is the best form of instruction.

三、开悟是最好的课程

还是"一切以学生为中心"！在我们的经验中，一般而言，越是自学能力强的人学习能力越好。那么一群高素养的成年人，在各自领域已经多有建树，如何激发自己的开悟更有意义？据统计，开悟本身的愉悦感持久性超过包括知识、性爱等在内的人类那些最美好体验。

这也是为什么选择"科学"来作为探索的主线。我们大多在管理、哲学、文学和艺术等方面浸染甚多，而不自觉地忽视了"科学的美妙"。科学其实也不一定总是晦涩无趣的，也有着很多"美的"和"妙的"！科学家的视野思维和思想，对于今天商业过载的中国来说，也是美的妙的美妙的！

我曾就此请教过湖畔大学的曾鸣教授，他说，湖畔沿着商业实践的路走，你们想沿着科学探索的路走，没有对错，大胆实践就好！我也主动和李善友教授创办的混沌大学合作过一期以科学为主题的硅谷课程，最近他在公开演讲中，提出以创新为主线办学，也是一条路。甚至近来很多人开始问我，GASA大学怎么与湖畔和混沌竞争？我认为我们根本不是对手，二位都是我敬佩的教授，我要学的还多着呢。我希望可以的话，和他们以及更多的人打造"中国大学的菜市场"，成行成市！大学这么多年来，在我国神圣到不可侵犯，以致这一百年似乎只有

This goes back again to our "student centered" approach. In our experience, the students who are able to teach themselves best are also those who are able to learn best. So then, when our students are a group of highly qualified adults who have already accomplished much in their respective fields, it would be most meaningful to ask how we can best help them achieve enlightenment. According to statistics, the sheer pleasure of enlightenment lasts much longer than pleasure brought by the acquisition of knowledge, sexual intercourse, and many other activities generally considered most pleasurable.

This is the reason we chose science as the focus of our curriculum. Most of us have been working and excelling in fields like management, philosophy, literature and art, but have ignored, without intending to, the unique beauty of science. Science is not always dense and dull. Indeed, it can be very beautiful and elegant as well. The unique visions and revolutionary thinking of scientists, in our much too commercial world, are beautiful and elegant as well.

I have consulted Prof. Zeng Ming of Hupan University on this topic. He said: "Hupan's curriculum focuses on practical and commercial subjects, while you want to pursue a more scientific path with GASA University. There is no right or wrong here, as long as you are bold in your exploration." I also took the initiative to collaborate on a course focused on science with Hundun University, which was founded by Professor Li Shanyou. Recently in a speech he gave, Prof. Li put forward the idea of forming universities that focus on innovation, which is also an interesting path. Recently, everyone has been asking me how GASA University can compete with Hupan University and Hundun University. But in fact, I do not consider them competitors. I greatly respect the founders of both of these institutions, and hope to learn from them instead of competing with them. If possible, I would like to collaborate with them and others to create a whole industry for higher education, with its own market and market rules. Higher education in China has always been sacred and inviolable to the point that

北大清华，大家还一直在诟病。

回来，关注学生的"开悟"，那我们怎样来开悟？我一向自诩是"世界小邮差"，还是把目光投向了这个世界，再小，也要是世界的！我们GASA大学2017级，未来三年，选择在世界八个国家和地区进行我们八期学习探索。开悟应具有多样性，这个世界是多元的，求同存异，建立自我，追求无我，不同国家和地区，不同文化，不同人情世故，都有益于开悟。

第一期求学探索地点选择美国，选择硅谷，我们探索科学和创新。随着人工智能时代的来临，人类空间探索方面的突破，我们相信硅谷仍然将引领这个世界的创新，越来越多科学家也开始在这儿大展拳脚。

第二期是印度。我们探索古印度文明，包括与中国渊源颇深的佛教以及快速成长的科技行业发展。我过去几年多次去印度，每次都在精神上有所启发，同时也惊叹这个国家的蓬勃发展。

第三期是以色列。创新和宗教。以色列小而美式的创新让人羡慕，三大宗教起源地耶路撒冷，你总能在不经意间陷入沉思。

only a few top universities like Peking University and Tsinghua University have flourished in the last hundred years or so, and even they have been criticized.

But let us return to the topic of "enlightenment"—how can we best enlighten our students? I have always considered myself a "Universal Postboy" (the English title was coined for me by Kai-fu Lee), so my view has always been a global one. Even if our school is still in its infancy and is small in scale for now, it belongs to the entire world. Our Class of 2017 will study in eight countries around world over the next three years. We believe that enlightenment should be diverse, just as our world is diverse. We should learn about those different from us, while work hard to discover ourselves, and finally to integrate into this multi-faceted world. All these different countries, cultures, and ways of living, will help bring about our enlightenment.

We will spend our first semester in Silicon Valley, in the U.S., where we will focus on science and innovation. As we welcome the Age of Artificial Intelligence, and witness the latest breakthroughs in science, we believe Silicon Valley is leading the world in terms of innovation, and more scientists than ever are on the cusp of accomplishing amazing things there.

Our second semester will be in India, where we will explore Ancient Indian culture, including Buddhism, which has played a major role in Chinese culture, as well as the rapidly expanding technology sector in India. I have visited India many times over the past few years. I have always found abundant inspiration there, and was often amazed by the vibrant development of the country.

Our third semester will be in Israel, where we will focus on innovation and religion. Israel has made enviable progress in its small but booming tech sector. And of course, when one visits Jerusalem, the birthplace of three major religions, one cannot help but contemplate the meaning of life, our vast universe, and many other topics.

此外，我们想更多探索日企的长久之道，英国的近现代的辉煌之路以及中国台湾的中华文化的传承，等等，即使巴西的亚马孙丛林也都会是我们的课堂！

No education, only learning!

文　厨

2017年6月18日于硅谷

不东 | UNIVERSAL POSTBOY

In addition, we will visit Japan and learn from the long-term visions of Japanese corporations, the glittering modern and contemporary development of the U.K., as well as the traditional Chinese heritage of Taiwan. We will even find much to learn from in the Amazons in Brazil.

As always: No education, only learning!

Wen Chu
June 18, 2017, Silicon Valley

GASA 大学

探索什么探索

时光荏苒，科学复兴硅谷一百天过去了。GASA大学硅谷第一期学习结束，不能寐，夜长思。

对于自己，对于这个时代，我到底在探索什么？见天地？见众生？见自己？我以为见到了天地，大江大河，群山巍峨，但穹顶之上，满天星辰，几无所知；我以为见到了众生，各种肤色，不同民族，但人情冷暖，洞察世事，一知半解；我以为见到了自己，趋利避害，沽名钓誉，但心如止水，浩然正气，用力不及。

这两年，我几乎穷极所能，借助我创办的长城会GMIC，我号叫"科学复兴"。觉得还不过瘾，发起GASA大学，践行使命，摆乎"No education, only learning"，美其名曰：无受教，唯探索。

那么，到底什么是探索呢？我一直想探索什么？而且过去

不东 | UNIVERSAL POSTBOY

The Meaning of "Exploration"

Time flies. The Scientific Renaissance Silicon Valley was hosted one hundred days ago. The first semester of GASA University Silicon Valley has ended as well. I have missed both deeply.

I ask myself, what am I exploring in this era, as well as in myself? The world? The people? Or myself? I believe that I have seen this world along with its myriad of rivers and mountains. However, I know almost nothing about the stars and the universe. I believe that I have seen the people of this world, with their different ethnicities and skin colors. However, I do not know nearly enough about their lives, or about the happiness and sadness they all experience each day. I believe I have seen my authentic self, because I have learned not to value worldly statuses or possessions. However, I have not worked nearly hard enough to have no desires, or to become a truly noble soul.

In the last two years, with the help of the GWC and the GMIC, I have poured all my resources and efforts into what I call the "Scientific Renaissance." I have also founded GASA University to realize my vision for education, which is "No education, only learning."

So then, what is exploration? I have been wanting to explore, and over the past

两年我很认真地去探索了,但可能一直没搞清楚什么是探索。

见霍金教授,探索科学精神,探索声名显赫,探索最强大脑……但为什么他躺在轮椅上,访谈结束时他的嘴角努力地挤出笑容来道别,这样的画面总是闪现在我的脑海?一个正常人,不要说一个天才,躺在轮椅上50年,还能如此乐观,这份乐观就是探索!

见佩雷斯先生,探索政要功绩,探索诺奖荣誉,探索安身立命……但为什么临别时,我调侃未来之我时,他露齿对视,开怀大笑,永远定格脑海?坦诚相待就是探索!

见理查德·沃曼先生,探索成功秘密,探索思想乐趣,探索特立独行……但一本本小册子,纯谈兴趣,不论销路,这份淡定,记忆深刻,或许这样的求知就是探索!

为此,未来几年,我想探索什么是探索。探索什么并不重要,探索什么探索更重要。

比如什么是财富?这个世界上最有财富的那几个人,我还是略有兴趣。

比如什么是权力?这个世界上那些政要,我准备酌情多见

two years, I have been exploring earnestly. However, I have never understood the meaning of exploration.

With Professor Stephen Hawking, I explored the spirit of science, what it is like to be known throughout the world, and the capabilities of an extraordinary mind. But I remember most of all the professor in his wheelchair, working hard to put a smile on to say goodbye to me at the end of our meeting. Putting aside his remarkable intellect, just as a person, it is amazing that he could be in a wheelchair for 50 years and stay optimistic. This optimism is exploration!

With President Shimon Peres, I explored his political achievements, his Nobel Prize, and his work in a turbulent environment. But I remember most of all when we were saying goodbye, and I was joking about my future, he laughed with me with such sincerity. I believe this sincere treatment of others is the meaning of exploration.

With Mr. Richard Wurman, I explored the secret of his success, the agility of his mind, and the way he always did his own thing. But I remember most of all his booklets that he wrote for interest, without any concern for sales. This thirst for knowledge is the meaning of exploration!

As a result of these wonderful meetings with these extraordinary people, in the next few years, I want to explore the meaning of exploration. It does not matter as much what one is exploring. It is most important to keep always this spirit of exploration.

What is wealth? I am interested in getting to know the wealthiest few in the world;

What is power? When I can, I want to meet the heads of states of this world. I

见。在此之前，书生意气，于我而言，政客如过江之鲫。现在我看，权力就是探索，未来数年，出入总统府邸、总理衙门、皇亲贵戚处所，非痴迷权力，乃探索。

比如什么是名声？学习佩雷斯先生的坦诚，目前我对于名声着实有兴致，这对我而言，马上就有很实际的效用。但我会对那些名声虽大，却大而低调到几乎人间蒸发的人尤其有兴致。

以上胡编乱造，也得感谢霍金教授，一个在轮椅上躺了50年的长者，如此乐观，我实在没有理由不努力乐观！

GASA大学我想找到3000名同学，作为第一个报名并被自己录取的学生，我想和你一起终生学习，见天地，见众生，见自己。我梦想成为这个时代的苏格拉底，如果最终我不是，同学中的你成为"他"，作为创办人和你的同学，我会更开心！因为这原本就是天意，绝非仅仅人力所致。

No education, only learning!

文　厨
GASA大学创办人2017年9月18日于硅谷

used to spurn meetings with politicians. But now, I understand that power is also exploration. In the next few years, I plan to meet with presidents and premiers, not out of adoration of power, but out of my love for exploration.

What is fame? Learning from President Peres' authenticity, I have a great interest in fame at the moment. To me, fame can be put to practical use right away. However, I am most interested in those who are famous, but who have nonetheless chosen to live life away from the public eye.

I must thank Professor Hawking for my rambling above. He has stayed optimistic through 50 years in a wheelchair. What reasons do I have for not being optimistic?

Allow me to insert a brief advertisement for those of you who have read this far. I want to seek 3,000 students for GASA University. As the first to enroll, I want to study with you, and learn about the world, the lives, and ourselves. I dream of becoming the Socrates of our era, but if in the end I do not attain this dream, I would love for one of you to become him. That would make me very happy, both as the founder of GASA University, and as your fellow classmate, because that would have been a decision made by the Divine.

No education, only learning!

Wen Chu
September 18, 2017, Founder of GASA University , Silicon Valley